THE DUEL IN MID-AIR.

Air Service Boys Over The Enemy's Lines

OR

The German Spy's Secret

BY

CHARLES AMORY BEACH

Author of "Air Service Boys Flying for France"

THE WORLD SYNDICATE PUBLISHING CO.
CLEVELAND, O.　　　　　NEW YORK, N. Y.

Copyright, MCMXIX, *by*
GEORGE SULLY & COMPANY

Printed in the United States of America
by
THE COMMERCIAL BOOKBINDING CO.
CLEVELAND, O.

AIR SERVICE BOYS OVER THE ENEMY'S LINE

CONTENTS

CHAPTER		PAGE
I.	Back of the Trenches	1
II.	The Winged Messenger	10
III.	A Spy Baffled	19
IV.	Praise from the General	27
V.	The Strange Warning	35
VI.	Looking Backward	45
VII.	The Great Day Arrives	53
VIII.	Over the Enemy's Lines	61
IX.	Winning His Spurs	70
X.	After the Battle	78
XI.	A Show on the Front	85
XII.	Clowns on the Wing	94
XIII.	More Work in Prospect	103
XIV.	Off on a Daring Mission	113
XV.	The Moonlight Flight	120
XVI.	Landing Close to Metz	129
XVII.	More Trouble for the Chums	137
XVIII.	The Lone House by the Roadside	144
XIX.	A Nest of Spies	153
XX.	Jack Climbs a Wall	162
XXI.	In the Old Lorraine Château	171

CONTENTS

CHAPTER	PAGE
XXII. FACING MORE DIFFICULTIES	181
XXIII. LEFT BEHIND IN THE ENEMY'S COUNTRY	191
XXIV. TROUBLOUS TIMES FOR JACK	200
XXV. BACK TO SAFETY—CONCLUSION	208

AIR SERVICE BOYS OVER THE ENEMY'S LINES

CHAPTER I

BACK OF THE TRENCHES

"Tom, what do you suppose that strange man who looked like a French peasant, yet wasn't one, could have been up to late yesterday afternoon?"

"You mean the fellow discovered near the hangars at the aviation camp, Jack?"

"Yes. He seemed to go out of sight like a wreath of smoke does. Why, if the ground had opened and swallowed him up, once the hue and cry was raised, he couldn't have vanished quicker. I wonder if what they say about him can be true?"

"That he was a German spy? Anything is possible in war times."

"I guess you're right there. German secret sympathizers, and spies in the bargain, seemed to bob up all over the United States before we crossed the ocean to do our fighting for France as aviators."

"They certainly were busy bees, Jack, blowing up munition-works, trying to destroy big railroad bridges so as to cripple traffic with the Allies over here; burning grain elevators in which France and Great Britain had big supplies of wheat stored; and even putting bombs aboard ocean liners that were timed to explode days later, when the boat would be a thousand miles from land."

"Over in France here they make short work of spies, I've heard, Tom!"

"Yes, it's a drumhead court martial and trial. Then, if the man or woman is found guilty, the spy goes out with a firing squad to the most convenient stone wall. They never return, Jack."

"Whee! that sounds like war times, doesn't it? And to think the two of us are right on the firing line, in the midst of all the scrapping. But, Tom, tell me, why should a tricky German spy want to hang out around the aviation field? He could hardly expect to pick up any news there that would be worth taking across the lines to the headquarters of the Crown Prince before Verdun."

"Don't be too sure of that, Jack. Perhaps he might learn of some contemplated bombing expedition, like that one we went on not so long ago." And Tom Raymond smiled slightly.

"They are a mighty clever bunch, those spies," admitted Jack Parmly.

"Why, Jack, half of the successes of the Kaiser's armies on all fronts, Russia, France and Rumania, can be laid at the door of his secret agents. They seem to be everywhere, trying to foment internal troubles, strikes, and discontent, so that when the Germans strike hard they meet a divided enemy in front."

"Well, I certainly wish we had caught that fellow."

"You were in the crowd, you told me, that scoured the whole neighborhood in search of him."

"That's right, I was. But say, he proved too foxy for us all. Anyway, we failed to find the rascal. Then night came on, when we had to give our man-hunt over. And to think that I even glimpsed the fellow's face in the bargain before the alarm went out!"

"Then you'd know him again perhaps, Jack, if ever you met him?"

"I think so. Though I suppose these spies have ways of changing their looks at times. But, to change the subject, Tom, it strikes me neither of us is groaning under the weight of game so far on our little side hunt." And Jack Parmly grinned.

"Oh, I didn't really expect to run across anything, though that French peasant assured us there were still some rabbits in the burrows over here, three miles back of our sleeping quarters. That's why, with a day off-duty, I took a notion to borrow an old Belgian-made double-barrel shotgun he owned, and walk out here."

"More to stretch our legs and get the kinks out, than anything else, eh, Tom?"

"That's it, Jack. Don't you remember that while we were training at the aviation school at Pau we used often to walk from the town, eight miles distant, until we sighted that famous little old red barn at Pau, where the Wright Brothers conducted some of their experiments in flying heavier-than-air machines. That was some little hike."

"Then too, Tom, I guess we wanted to get together by ourselves for a change, so we could talk about our folks at home in little old Bridgeton, U. S. A.," went on Jack Parmly with a sigh. "All the fellows of the Lafayette Escadrille are mighty kind and sociable, but there are times when a fellow gets homesick. Just remember that we have been over here many months now. It seems years to me, Tom."

"Say, I hope you are not homesick enough to want to go back, old fellow?"

"Not me, Tom. I made up my mind to stick

it out until we whip the Kaiser. But already I can see it'll never be an accomplished fact until Uncle Sam throws his sword into the scales. And any day now something may drop."

"Yes, matters are at an acute stage in Washington, that's sure. All France, bled nearly white in two-and-a-half years of war, is praying that the day may come soon."

After that the two athletic looking young Americans, dressed in the uniform of the French aviation corps, fell silent for a brief time. They, however, continued to trudge over the devastated fields, looking this way and that for any sign of a stray rabbit that had escaped the general slaughter.

It was just previous to the world-stirring session of Congress, when the President made his thrilling speech that sounded almost from end to end of the world, and put America in line for the cause of democracy. Anxious days those were across the ocean, anxious not only in France, Italy and Great Britain, in Serbia, Rumania, Greece and Russia, but in the Central Empires, also.

For well did those in Teutonic authority know, in spite of their vain boasting, that once great America decided, the thing was bound to be done, sooner or later. Never in the course of her history has our republic been on a losing side. Her wars have invariably brought eventual victory to her arms, because she has never once fought for an unjust cause.

These two vigorous young fellows were fair samples of those enterprising Americans who found it impossible to sit idly by. They could not await the slow course of events that was bound to carry our country into the world war on the side of the Allies, in spite of all the powerful counter currents among the pro-German citizens at home.

Dozens of the brightest of flying men from the States had gone over and offered their services to France, the country they loved. In time there came to be so many, that from the ordinary French Flying Corps there was formed a unit entirely made up of Americans.

This, in honor of the one great Frenchman whom Americans most honor at home, was called the Lafayette Escadrille. Some of its members had become famous at their profession. Names like those of Lufbery, Thaw, McConnell, Chapman, Prince, Rockwell, Hill, Rumsey, Johnson, Balsley and others became household words among readers of the great dailies in the States.

Tom Raymond was the son of a man who had gained fame as an inventor. When the war broke out he started work on numerous inventions, some of which were calculated to become terrible agents for the destruction of human life. Then Mr. Raymond's mood changed, and he set to work to conceive a wonderful stabilizer for airplane use that would save myriads of lives, and if adopted by Uncle Sam was likely to help win the war for the Allies.

Just when this invention was finished a drawing of one of the parts was stolen by a German spy. Later on, after Tom and his chum, Jack Parmly had decided to become war aviators, having already had considerable aviation experience, they went to the flying school conducted by the Government in Virginia.

From there in course of time they crossed the Atlantic and entered the famous French school at Pau. Then, having mastered the science of flying sufficiently to be sent to the front, they had joined the Lafayette Escadrille, as related in a previous volume entitled "Air Service Boys Flying for France; or The Young Heroes of the Lafayette Escadrille."

Tom in particular seemed to have a great career ahead of him, unless some unfortunate accident, or possibly a Teuton pilot, cut it short, as had happened in the cases of Rockwell, Prince, McConnell and Chapman. Every one knew he possessed genius of a high order, and that it would not be long before Tom Raymond might anticipate gaining the proud title of "*ace*," which would indicate that he had defeated five enemies at different times, and put them entirely out of the running.

Tom was already a corporal in the French service, and expected before a great while to be given the privilege of wearing the chevrons of a sergeant. Jack had not progressed so rapidly but was doing well.

And now to return to the young aviators during their walk.

"I reckon we've gone far enough, Jack," Tom remarked presently. "Our friend Jean may have been telling the truth when he said there were still a few bunnies left alive in this war-racked section of country, but I can see they've got the good sense to stick to their burrows during the daytime. We won't be burdened with our bag of game on the return trip."

"Yes, that's always the trouble, when you go out after rabbits and haven't any hound along to get them up and bring them within gunshot," grumbled Jack.

"But we've had a good walk," returned his companion; "and for a time we managed to get away from that terrible explosion of shells, and big-gun firing. We ought to be thankful for our little time off, Jack."

"Oh! I'm not really complaining," remarked

the other young aviator, with a whimsical expression on his good-natured face. "But don't you know I hate to go back without having fired even one shot." He stopped short and pointed upward. "Hold on, Tom; there's some kind of bird going to pass over right now! Crow or anything, please bring it down! I'll promise to eat it, no matter what it is."

Laughingly Tom threw the gun up to his shoulder, and the next instant the report sounded. It seemed almost contemptible, after listening to the roar of those monster shells exploding for so long.

The bird fell fluttering in a heap. Tom evidently was a fair marksman, for it had been moving swiftly over their heads at the time he fired. Jack ran forward and picked the game up. As he did so he gave utterance to exclamations that naturally excited the curiosity of his chum. So Tom, after reloading his gun with a fresh shell, waited for Jack to rejoin him, which the other did, his face full of mystery.

CHAPTER II

THE WINGED MESSENGER

"What do you call this, Tom? A queer sort of crow, I'd say. Looks more to me like the blue-rock pigeons Sam Becker used to raise at home," and so saying Jack held up the still quivering bunch of feathers.

Tom took one quick look, and then a startled expression flitted across his face.

"Just what it is, Jack!" he hastened to say. "A homing pigeon in the bargain! You can tell that from the bill and the ring around the eyes."

Jack in turn became aroused.

"A homing pigeon, is it?" he ejaculated. "Why, birds like that are used for carrying messages across the lines! Some of our airplane pilots have told me that sometimes they take a French spy far back of the German front. When he had made an important discovery he would write a message in cipher, enclose it in a tiny waterproof capsule attached to a ring about the pigeon's leg, and set the bird free. Inside of half an hour it would be safe back in its loft, and the message on the way to French headquarters."

He lifted one limp leg, and then the other.

"Look here, it's got a message, as sure as anything!" Jack exclaimed.

Tom leaned forward and took the bird in his hand, dropping the gun meanwhile. He carefully took off the gelatine capsule, and from it extracted a delicate piece of tough paper, which he spread open. There were a series of strange marks on the paper, of which neither of the air service boys could make anything.

"Looks like hieroglyphics, such as you'd expect to find on an Egyptian tomb or in the burial places under the pyramids," complained Jack, after he had stared at the lines in disgust for a brief period of time.

"It's a cipher of some kind," explained Tom, seriously. "With the key all this would resolve itself into some sort of communication, I suppose, connected with valuable information concerning the French armies here at Verdun."

"Then it was made by a spy!"

"No question about that part of it," came the ready reply.

"This carrier pigeon with this message, was on its way across to some point in the rear of the enemy line when you fired, and brought the poor little thing down in a quivering heap, I'm sure that's it," continued the other.

"Yes. And so after all it's turned out to

be a lucky thing you chanced to see the bird coming along, Jack, and begged me to knock it down so we could show some sort of game when we got back to camp."

"What ought we do with this message?" asked Jack, accustomed to depending on his more energetic chum in many cases; though when left to his own resources he could think for himself, as had frequently been proved.

"I shall see that it gets to French headquarters, with an account of the singular way we ran across it," Tom told him.

"Do you think it would be possible for any one there to translate this cipher of the German secret code?"

"Why not?" Tom demanded. "They are clever people, these wideawake French, and I shouldn't be at all surprised if they turned this incident to some good use."

"How?"

"Oh, it could be done in many ways. Suppose they found the key to the code. Don't you see how a fictitious message could be sent on in some way, if they could bag another pigeon from the same coop? They might even coax the Germans to deliver a furious attack at a supposed weak place in the line, which would of course be heavily guarded."

"That would be something worth while!" exclaimed the other with glowing eyes. "Lead them into a trap, where they would be mowed down like ripe grain, terrible as that sounds!"

"Yes, that's the idea I had in mind. But it would depend on several things. First of all would come the successful solving of this cipher code."

"Yes, and then the finding of another homing pigeon," added Jack. "I wonder if the fellow who released that bird could have a lot more of the same kind hidden away somewhere around back here."

"I was just going to suggest that we take a turn toward the south, and look around a bit before going back to camp. Do you feel equal to it, Jack?"

"What, me! Tom? Why, I'm as fresh as a daisy! This business has made me forget there's such a thing as getting tired walking."

"Let's see, we stood here when I fired," continued Tom reflectively, "and you walked straight to where the bird dropped. That would make the direction due northwest by southeast. How about that, Jack?"

The other took a survey, and then pointed with his hand.

"When I saw the bird coming first of all, Tom," he finally remarked, "it was just showing up over that clump of trees killed by gunfire.

And it was heading as straight as can be for us."

"Yes," Tom went on to say, "because a homing pigeon on being released will rise to a certain height and take its bearings. Then it starts in a bee-line for its loft, whether that is five miles away or hundreds of miles. Some peculiar instinct tells it in which way home lies. It seldom if ever goes astray. Sometimes birds have made a thousand miles, and shown up at their home coop days after being set free."

"Well, then, the man who threw it into the air, after fastening this cipher message to it, must be over to the southeast of us," affirmed Jack.

"The bird was released within five minutes or so of the time I fired," Tom told his chum. "It's even possible the spy may have heard the report of my gun."

"Tom, why not try to capture that spy?" asked Jack, eagerly, ready for any sort of excitement.

The young aviators started off, walking briskly. They kept their eyes alertly open as they proceeded. At the same time, on Tom's suggestion, they continued to act as though still looking for game, even investigating at a burrow that certainly was used by rabbits, as the tracks plainly indicated.

Tom never deviated from a direct line due southeast. He knew that their best chance of making a valuable discovery lay in finding the place where the carrier pigeon had been released, to fly across the lines to its home loft. This might be many miles to the rear of the fighting front, even on Lorraine territory, in the neighborhood of the fortified city of Metz itself.

The two passed over a mile without making any sort of discovery, Jack, who did not possess quite as determined a nature as his comrade, was already commencing to make certain sounds akin to complainings, as though he felt keenly disgruntled because of their lack of success.

"Guess we'll have to give it up, Tom," he finally remarked.

"Wait," said Tom. "Before doing that let's investigate that old shattered farmhouse over yonder."

"Hello!" exclaimed Jack, plucking up some fresh interest, "have you located one of those remains of a building, then? I was coming to believe there wasn't so much as a broken wall left standing for a space of five square miles, so complete has been the destruction. But I see what you mean, Tom."

They walked ahead again, and approached

the ruined farmhouse. It had been riddled through and through by shot and shell. Three-fourths of the original building lay in piles, the stones heaped up as they had fallen.

"Queer, isn't it, that the kitchen part escaped the smashing fire, and still stands," observed Jack. "I warrant you this is the only part of a building left around here. Tom, would our spy be likely to take up his headquarters in such a place as this, do you think?"

"I don't know," came the answer. "We can soon find out."

"He might feel desperate enough to open fire on us," suggested Jack, though he did not shrink or hold back when Tom advanced; for Jack Parmly did not have a drop of cowardly blood in his veins.

Tom turned and waved his hand as though beckoning to others who might be coming after them. He even called out in his best French, as if there were a dozen back of him that there was a possibility of securing at least a drink of cold water at the old-fashioned well with a sweep that stood near the kitchen of the ruined farmhouse.

"Good idea, Tom!" commented the other, chuckling with amusement. "If he gets the notion in his head that we are legion he won't be so apt to blaze away at us, knowing it would

THE WINGED MESSENGER 17

mean a short shrift for him. He may prefer to play the poor French peasant part, and try to pull the wool over our eyes."

Presently they arrived at the door. It was hanging from one hinge, and the entire place presented a vivid picture of the utter desolation cruel war always brings in its train.

Tom's first act before entering was to look down at the ground just before the door. Some intuition told him that if the place had been recently occupied they would possibly find some evidences of the fact in the earth.

"See there, Jack!" he suddenly exclaimed, as he pointed down close to his feet. "Fresh tracks, and made by a man's shoes in the bargain!"

"Some one has been in here for a fact, Tom, and I wouldn't be afraid to wager he saw us coming and cleared out in a hurry. He could have skirted those bushes, and got clear easy enough. Do you think it could have been the same chap who freed that pigeon?"

"No doubt about it," and Tom, stooping, picked up some small object. "See, here's a feather that was sticking to that dead weed. It's from a bird of the same color as the pigeon, perhaps from the very one I've got in my pocket."

"That settles it," snapped the pleased Jack.

"I must say you're a clever hand at finding these things out. I'd have never dreamed of looking down at my feet, but blundered right into the shack to see if—— Oh! What do you think of the luck we're in this day, Tom? See what stands there on that poor old three-legged table!"

Jack's excitement was natural, as Tom readily understood when he looked; for there was a small basket or cage made from oziers or willow wands; and inside this they could see two blue gray homing pigeons, mates to the one Tom had shot only a short time before!

CHAPTER III

A SPY BAFFLED

BOTH young aviators stared at the wicker cage containing the two pigeons. The birds had been still up to then, but now commenced to make cooing sounds, as though pleased at having human company. Apparently they were inclined to be sociable, as Jack afterwards put it.

"So he discovered us coming along," Jack went on to say, "and skipped out in such a hurry he didn't have time to carry away the cage with him."

"He must have climbed out of this window in the side of the wall," observed Tom. "We could have seen him if he had used the door. Yes, there are footprints underneath the window. He ran down behind those bushes and reached the stone wall that leads to the broken country and what is left of the woods."

"The chances are he had all that mapped out beforehand," suggested Jack. "Surely a spy has always to keep a door open for retreat."

"Yes. Why not? They take their lives in their hands every time they enter the hostile lines, and you can't blame a man for wanting to live a little longer, especially if he believes he can serve his country."

"Perhaps he hasn't got such a good start but that we could overtake him if we went after him now," suggested Jack.

"We might take a turn that way," his chum agreed. "But not too far afield. We didn't start out to search for spies, and we've only got a single gun between us. Even my automatic was left behind, because I didn't expect to have any use for it, and get tired carrying the thing, with its belt."

"But these pigeons here, Tom?"

"We can leave them until we get back. That's one reason why I don't want to get out of sight of the place. He might make a round, and carry the birds away while we were engaged in a hunt half a mile off. And it may be of much more importance that those live birds arrive in the French camp than that we should bag the spy."

"I get you, Tom; so let's commence our little man-hunt right away."

The two friends set off. Tom tried to follow the course he believed the spy must have taken on quitting the old farmhouse ruins. That his reckoning was clear he proved several times by pointing out to his companion plain evidences that some other person had passed along the way before them.

Here the marks of shoes could be detected in the soft earth. A little further on, and at a point where the man must have crawled in order to keep from being seen, they found tracks where his toes had dragged along, as well as the indentation of his knees in the soil.

Presently they arrived at the terminus of the stone wall, about the only thing remaining intact connected with the French farm. There was not a single tree showing signs of life in that patch of sombre forest; where shell-fire had failed to do the work of destruction a malicious hand had girdled the trunk with a keen-edged tool, and thus encompassed the doom of the trees.

Tom came to a pause.

"I reckon we've come far enough," he said, taking a look over toward the fragment of a house on the slight elevation, which could just be seen from their present position.

"I'd have liked to catch up with that duck and march him back to camp, along with his feathered messengers," Jack grumbled disappointedly. "Somehow I hate and despise a spy above all created things."

The youths set their faces once more in the direction of the ruins, where they soon arrived.

Jack half feared that in spite of them the cage and its feathered inmates had been spirited away. He hastened inside ahead of his companion and then called out cheerily:

"It's all right, Tom, and nobody at home. Here's the wicker cage and the pigeons, just as we left them!"

"As the afternoon is passing, and we have a long distance to go, we'd better be making a start," Tom remarked, when he reached the open door.

"Let me carry the pigeon cage, Tom, as you have the gun," suggested Jack, after slipping his hand through the ring at the top. "Say, perhaps the boys won't give us a laugh, to see what queer game we've brought back from our hunt!"

They left the ruins of the once peaceful farmhouse behind them, and commenced retracing their steps. Tom was too old a hand at hunting to get lost. He had kept his bearings through the whole tramp, no matter how many turns they took in examining some promising ground where rabbit burrows might be found. On this account then he would have no difficulty whatever in leading his comrade straight back to the villa in which the entire Lafayette Escadrille of American fliers was quartered.

They were passing along about half a mile

from the wrecked farmhouse kitchen, and not far from the spot where Tom made his successful shot, when without warning the report of a gun came to their ears. Jack involuntarily ducked his head.

"Say, did you hear that whining sound just over us, Tom? That was caused by a bullet skipping past!"

Tom for answer dragged his chum down behind a fringe of dead bushes that chanced to lie close by.

"It was a bullet, all right, Jack," he replied, not without a tremor in his voice, for this thing of being made a target by some murderous unseen person was a new and novel experience.

"Do you suppose it was fired by the man who owns these pigeons?" further questioned Jack, though showing no intention of loosening his grip on the wicker cage.

"It could hardly be any one else. He has dogged us this far, or else just happened to catch sight of us. That shot was fired from a distance, and if we take a notion to run he couldn't possibly hit us. But we might as well make use of this fringe of bushes to creep some way off. Then we'll get on our feet and put out for home at full speed."

This they proceeded to do without further delay. When it was no longer possible to utilize the bushes for cover, they sprang to their feet and ran. Jack fully anticipated hearing other shots—yes, and perhaps having more leaden missiles singing their vicious songs about his head. But he was agreeably disappointed in his expectations, for not a report came.

Evidently the spy had gone away, thinking discretion the better part of valor. He may have noticed that they were in uniform, and armed in the bargain.

Later on the air service boys moderated their mad pace, and as there seemed to be no further signs of danger they finally fell into a walk. Still neither of them lagged, but kept up a brisk pace, Jack casting numerous apprehensive glances over his shoulder, haunted by a lingering suspicion that the spy might yet give them trouble.

They came through safely at last. The villa in which the American fliers were quartered was reached, and seemed to be deserted at that hour in the afternoon. Everybody must be busy at the front, the boys concluded, for the din was more distracting than usual.

"We picked out a bad day for getting off, I'm afraid, Tom," Jack sighed. "They told us there was nothing big in prospect; but since we started out on our hunt I guess the Huns have put up something of size. And the boys will be in the thick of it all too! We might have had a share if we'd been on duty to-day."

"Brace up, Jack," chided his chum. "For all you know, what we've done may turn out to be ten times more important than all the work of the entire escadrille to-day. These captured birds and that cipher message, represent possibilities beyond anything you or I can know. Leave all that to the general."

"When do you mean to see him, Tom?"

"As soon as I can arrange it. And you're coming with me when I get the summons to his headquarters, depend on that, Jack. Your part in this affair is just as important as mine."

Tom put the cage with its cooing inmates in their room. Then he started out to try to get into communication with the commanding general. He had met him once by mere chance, but he hardly believed General Petain would remember him in the least.

The action was about over for the day. The Crown Prince had once again thrown a heavy storming party forward in the endeavor to make a breach in the French lines, through which he could pour the veteran reserves he had in waiting. But, as had often happened before, he counted without his host; and when the sun went down all he had to show for his stroke was a greatly increased casualty list.

The French could not be moved.

Tom understood how to go about it, and in the end managed to get an obliging French, captain whom he knew very well, to carry a message to the commander-in-chief to the effect that he had news of great importance to communicate. Just as Tom expected would be the case, this brought back a speedy answer.

"You are both to come with me, young Messieurs," said the captain, his eyes sparkling with interest, for Tom had told him enough to excite his curiosity, and he knew the Americans would not aimlessly take up the precious time of the general. "Our valiant commander is tired after a strenuous day; but never is he too weary to attend to duty; and he already finds himself interested in everything you brave young airmen attempt. So please accompany me to headquarters."

Shortly afterwards the boys found themselves face to face with General Petain.

CHAPTER IV

PRAISE FROM THE GENERAL

GENERAL PETAIN received the pair with his accustomed kindness. He loved youth, and his eyes sparkled with pleasure as he gave each of them a hand.

"My time is limited, I regret to say, my gallant Americans, or I should gladly ask you all manner of questions concerning your own country. We are all anxious to know when the great republic across the sea will decide to cast her decisive influence into the scales to bring us the victory we await with much patience. Tell me now what this strange thing is you have come across to-day."

Tom waited for no second bidding. He realized how tired the general must be after a strenuous day in keeping his finger on the pulse of the whole front, where the fierce German attacks had been hurled without success.

Accordingly he started at once his tale of how they had been given a day off for rest, and, having a love for hunting in their veins, had borrowed an old shotgun and started forth. Without wasting any time in useless descriptions he quickly reached the point where the pigeon was shot.

Jack, having nothing to say just then, contented himself with watching the various shades of expression that flitted across the face of the commander. At mention of the pigeon his eyes sparkled, and he leaned forward with an air of expectancy, as though anticipating what would come next.

Then, as Tom produced the message written on the thin but tough paper and handed it to the general the French officer eagerly scanned it. Jack also noticed that he did not appear disappointed because he could not immediately read the baffling communication. Of course it would be written in some secret code; that was to be expected.

"It is fortunate," remarked the French officer, "that I have on my staff one who is considered an expert at solving any and every species of cipher code. He will speedily figure it all out for me, and then we shall see what news this spy was transmitting to his commander. Please continue your story, which is very interesting, and in which your part does you both credit."

Tom, thus encouraged, went on. He told of their further search for the mysterious man who had set the homing pigeon free after attaching the secret message to it.

When he presently told of coming on the ruined farmhouse, and discovering the ozier cage containing two additional pigeons, just where the spy had left them in his hurried flight, the general fairly beamed.

"It is splendid news you have brought me—you aviators from our sister republic across the sea." he remarked exultantly, as though already in his fertile mind he could see great possibilities looming up whereby those pigeons might be made to serve a purpose.

The story was soon finished. Tom, of course, thought it necessary to tell of having been fired on while on their way back to the aviation post, though no harm had resulted. He did this not for the purpose of impressing the general with the idea that they had run any great personal risk, but because it might have some influence on the plans the officer probably had in mind.

After all had been told the commander again shook hands with both of the air service boys. This indicated, as Tom well knew, that he had given them all the time he could spare and that a dozen important things were awaiting his attention, so he saluted and turned to depart.

"This may prove to be a most important thing you have discovered," the general halted the aviators to say warmly. "The cipher will be solved, and then, if the facts warrant it, we may have another written that can be sent forward by one of your birds. You will give them over into the charge of an officer whom I shall dispatch back with you to your quarters. That will be convenient, I suppose?"

Tom hastened to assure him that they had expected just such a thing, and had hoped that the two captured pigeons might prove the means of leading the Crown Prince's forces into some sort of trap.

The general's black eyes snapped on hearing Tom say this.

"Ah! I see that you too have thought it out!" he exclaimed enthusiastically. "Some day perhaps you may have command of an army, and exercise that talent with glorious success. France thanks you."

Both boys were deeply moved by their brief interview with the busy commander-in-chief of the French forces. They did not feel any humiliation at being addressed as "my children," knowing that it was a term of endearment used freely by officers high in command when addressing those in the ranks. In fact, the French army is very much like a big family, the men loving those they serve under.

"Well, that job's over," remarked Jack, heaving a sigh of relief when they were on their way to their quarters, accompanied by a jaunty captain who, Tom believed, must be a member of the general's staff.

"I'm glad to have had such a fine opportunity for meeting General Petain," Tom returned, for the captain at the time was walking a little in the rear, conversing with a courier who had come running after him, as if on important business.

"He was fine, wasn't he, Tom?"

"Next to Joffre I understand General Petain is the most beloved commander the army has ever had," replied the other. "I'll always feel proud that he shook hands so heartily with both of us."

The air service boys were soon in the automobile that had carried them to the general's headquarters back of the French lines. Here the captain joined them, having finished his hasty consultation with the courier. On the ride to the aviation camp he chatted pleasantly with the young Americans. He, it appeared, had spent several years attached to the French Embassy at Washington.

He asked particularly concerning the feeling of the common people in America, and what influence the powerful cliques of naturalized but pro-German citizens were apt to have on the Government.

Tom was able to assure him that slowly but

surely the people of free America were becoming aroused to the deadly menace of German imperialism, and that presently—it might come at any day, according to the latest advices—Congress would assemble to hear a ringing appeal from the President, urging them to declare war upon the Kaiser, war to the finish.

Apparently what the boys said had much in it to comfort the French captain. He knew only too well how eagerly his wearied nation was listening to hear just such a message of hope. He knew, also, just what it would mean for the brave defenders of France.

In due time the three arrived at the villa. Several of the American pilots saw the trio leave the car, wondered much what was in the wind that Tom and Jack should return with a member of General Petain's personal staff. Their curiosity was considerably heightened when later they saw the captain come out of the villa carrying a small ozier cage containing two blue-rock carrier pigeons, and effusively shake hands with both Tom and Jack, calling out to them as the car moved off:

"In the name of France and General Petain I thank you for what you have done this day, my brave Americans!"

As the chums were about to pass into the building there was a hail.

PRAISE FROM THE GENERAL 33

"Wait a minute, Jack!" called one of their fellow pilots, hurrying up with some object in his hand at which the two boys stared with rising curiosity. I've got something here for you!"

"For me?" cried the youth addressed. "I'm ever so much obliged, but it strikes me I've got beyond the point of playing with a toy balloon; though honestly now, when I was a kid I used to be pretty fond of sailing one of 'em at the end of a long string, until it would get away, and leave me staring up while it climbed toward the clouds."

"Oh, this one is about past doing any climbing, I should say," replied the pilot, laughing at Jack's description of his childish woes. "In fact, it's been out during the night, and the heavy air forced it to come down. Listen, and I'll tell you a strange story that will make you believe in fairy tales."

"Go on then, please," urged Jack. "You've got me all worked up already. So there's a history attached to this little balloon, is there?"

"There was *something* attached to it, something that may mean much or little to you fellows," came the reply. "This thing was found by a French dispatch bearer on his way across country. Out of curiosity he stepped aside to look at the bobbing red object he had noticed among some bushes in an open field. When he found that it had a paper fastened to it, which on the outside had an address, he concluded to bring the whole business along with him. He came here half an hour back inquiring for Jack Parmly, and on finding you were away at the time left the balloon and the paper in my charge. Take it, and see what the message is, Jack!"

CHAPTER V

THE STRANGE WARNING

"Open it, Jack, and see what the message is," urged Tom, as his chum stood with the scrap of damp paper held between his fingers, having allowed the sagging little toy balloon to fall at his feet.

Jack was thinking just at that moment of the other message his companion and he had found attached to the homing pigeon. But of course they could not possibly have any sort of connection!

He opened the small bit of paper. It had some writing in lead pencil. Once it had doubtless been plain enough, but the dampness must have caused it to become faint. Still, Jack could make it out without much difficulty. This was what he read aloud, so that Tom and the other pilot could hear:

"Look carefully to your planes; examine every part. There is treachery in the air!"

"That's all, fellows," said Jack, much puzzled, as he turned the paper over and over, looking for some signature.

"No name attached, Jack?" asked his chum.

"Nothing whatever to tell who wrote that warning. Here, take a look at it, Tom. Your eyes may be sharper than mine and see something I've missed."

But Tom and the other pilot both failed to throw any light on the matter after examining the paper thoroughly. They exchanged stares. Then Jack laughed, a little queerly.

"This is certainly a mystery," he went on to say, trying to take the thing as a joke. "Some kind friend sends me a solemn warning, and then neglects to sign his name. Do you think any of the fellows of the escadrille could be up to a prank?"

Tom shook his head. The other pilot also exhibited positive signs of doubt in connection with such a thing.

"The boys often have their little jokes, and we are a merry bunch much of the time, just to change off from the nervous strain we're living under," the man observed. "But I'm sure not one of them would dream of doing a thing like this. It would be a mean trick."

"Then both of you are inclined to believe this warning was meant in all seriousness, are you?" continued Jack, no longer grinning as before.

"Yes, I do," Tom instantly announced. "It seems a bit childish, sending it in such a queer fashion; but then perhaps it was the only way open to the person. There was one chance in ten that it would be found; but you know sometimes we can't choose our way of doing things, but must accommodate ourselves to circumstances. This toy balloon being handy suggested a possible way of getting the warning to you, Jack."

"But why me any more than you, Tom, or any other fellow in the escadrille?" continued Jack, sorely bewildered.

"That's something we can only guess at," he was told. "Evidently this person had your name, and knew you were working here with the Lafayette boys. Try to think of some one you may have done something for to make him feel grateful to you. Could it have been that boyish-looking German prisoner we talked with the other day, and for whom you bound up a badly damaged arm, Jack?"

"Oh! that boy!" exclaimed the other, and then shook his head. "No, it's impossible. You see the poor chap could hardly talk halfway decent English, and I'm sure he never could write my name like this. Besides, Tom," Jack went on triumphantly, "I never bothered to mention to him that I had a name. To him I was simply an American flying for France."

"Anybody else you can think of?" persisted

Tom, for it seemed to him that it meant considerable to try to discover who had sent the message by such a strange channel.

Jack pondered. Then all at once he looked up with a light in his eyes.

"You've thought of something!" exclaimed the other pilot eagerly.

"Well, it might be possible, although I hardly believe she'd be the one to go to such trouble. Still, she had children, she told me, at her home in Lorraine, back of Metz; and this is a child's toy, this little hot-air balloon."

"Do you mean that woman you assisted a week or so ago? Mrs. Neumann?" asked Tom, quickly.

"Yes, it was only a little thing I was able to do for her, but she seemed grateful, and said she hoped some day to be in a position to repay the favor. Then later on I learned she had secured permission to cross over to the German lines, in order to get to her family. She is a widow with six children, you know, a native of Lorraine, and caught by accident in one of the sudden furious rushes of the French, so that she had been carried back with them when they retreated. At the time she had been serving as a Red Cross nurse among the Germans. It was on that account the French allowed her to return to her family. They are very courteous, these French."

Tom was listening. He nodded his head as though it seemed promising at least.

"Let's figure it out," he mused. "Which way was the wind coming from last night, do either of you happen to know?"

"Almost from the north," the other aviator instantly responded. "I chanced to notice that fact, for other reasons. But then it was almost still, so the little balloon could not have drifted many miles before the heavy atmosphere dragged it down until finally it landed in the field."

"Well, that settles one thing," asserted Tom. "It came from back of the German lines, don't you see?"

"Yes, that seems probable," admitted Jack.

"Your unknown friend was there at the time," continued Tom, in his lawyer-like way, following up the trail he had started; "and hence apparently in a position to know that some sort of plot was being engineered against one Jack Parmly. Don't ask me why *you* should be selected for any rank treachery, because I don't know."

"And this person, this unknown friend of mine," Jack added, "wishing to warn me so that I might not meet a bad end to-day, sent out this message in the hope that it might fall back of our lines and be picked up. Tom, it makes me have a queer feeling. I almost think I must be asleep and dreaming."

"No, it's real enough. We may never know who the writer of this note is; but we can heed the warning just the same, and go over to examine our planes minutely. Whoever it was, spelled your name correctly. I've studied the writing, but it seems to be assumed, and clumsy. There was a reason for that too, as well as the writer failing to sign a name."

"What sort of reason?" queried Jack.

"Fear that in some way the message, and the balloon, might fall into German hands and lead to unpleasant results," Tom continued. "We know about how those Huns would serve any one who tried to spoil their plans. They believe in frightfulness every time, and it might mean death to the writer. This she evidently knew full well."

"Just why do you say 'she' when you speak of the writer?"

"Oh, I have an idea that Mrs. Neumann may be the mysterious friend who is taking such desperate chances to send you a warning. Anyway, something about it seems to say it isn't a man's handwriting. Besides, neither of you may have noticed it, but there's a faint odor, as of

THE STRANGE WARNING 41

perfume, adheres to that bit of paper, though the dampness has taken it almost all out."

Jack looked astonished at such shrewd reasoning.

"Well, you are certainly a wonder at seeing through things, Tom," he hastened to say. "And so of course that settles it in my mind. Mrs. Neumann sent this message to me; though how she could have learned that there was anything treacherous going on beats my powers of reasoning."

"But don't you think it would pay to learn if there's any truth about it all?" asked the other pilot, whose curiosity had been stirred up by such a strange happening.

"Yes, let's all go over to the hangars and have the planes out for a regular inspection," said Tom. "If mischief has been done the chances are it would be in a part not usually examined by the machanician before a flight. Then again the damage, if there is any, might be so covered up by the shrewd schemer that it would not be noticeable."

There were always cars going to and fro, for pilots came and went from time to time; so the trio quickly found themselves being whirled along over the road so often traveled in their daily work.

"How about that fellow they chased late yesterday afternoon, who was loitering about the hangars and acting in a suspicious way?" asked the friendly pilot, as they rode along. "More than a few of the fellows say he must have been a spy, and up to some mischief, because he slipped off so slickly."

"I had him in mind all the while," said Tom. "And if any mischief has been done, of course we can lay it at his door; though just how he managed to work we'll perhaps never know."

"I caught sight of him, too," Jack remarked; "and I only wish now I'd had a good look at the chap who owned those pigeons to-day, so as to tell if they were one and the same, which I believe to be a fact."

Just then Tom gave his chum a kick with the toe of his shoe. This suddenly reminded Jack that he was treading on forbidden ground, since they had resolved not to say anything to a third person concerning the adventure of that afternoon.

The other member of the escadrille was looking interested. He understood that Tom and Jack must have met with some singular adventure; but since they did not see fit to take him into their confidence he was too polite to ask questions, feeling there must be a good reason for their silence.

Presently they arrived at the hangars. It was

THE STRANGE WARNING 43

now almost sunset. The fliers were coming down one by one, their labor for the day having been accomplished. It had been a pretty arduous day, too, and two members of the escadrille had new honors coming to them, since they had dropped enemy planes in full view of tens of thousands of cheering spectators, after thrilling combats high in the air.

One had also passed through an experience that few aviators can look back to. He had started to drop rapidly when, at almost ten thousand feet altitude, his motor was struck by a missile from a rival pilot's gun. When halfway down, either through a freak of fortune or some wonderfully clever manipulation on the part of the pilot, the machine righted, and he was enabled to volplane to safety, though considerably bruised and cut up through hasty landing.

Jack quickly had his little Nieuport out of the hangar, and the three airmen began a minute inspection. For a short time nothing developed that had a suspicious appearance. Jack, in fact, was beginning to believe the warning might after all be in the nature of a fake, or else the spy had not found a favorable chance to do his foul work before being frightened off.

But presently Tom gave utterance to an exclamation.

"Found anything, Tom?" asked Jack eagerly.

"Yes. Come around here, both of you!"

When the others joined Tom he pointed to where an important wire stay had been dextrously filed so that it must snap under a severe wrench or strain, such as commonly comes when a pilot is far afield, and wishes to execute a necessary whirl.

Jack shivered as he took in the meaning of that partly severed stay. If it gave way while he was far above the earth it must spell his certain doom!

CHAPTER VI

LOOKING BACKWARD

"Just see the fiendish cleverness of the fellow who filed that stay!" Tom cried, as they all stared. "He filled the indentation his sharp file made with a bit of wax or chewing-gum of the same general color. Why, no one would ever have noticed the least thing wrong when making the ordinary examination."

"Then how did you manage to find it, Tom?" asked Jack, breathing hard, as he pictured to himself the narrow escape he had had.

"I suspected something of the kind might be done; so I ran my thumb-nail down each wire stay," came the answer. "And it turned out just as I thought."

"There may be still more places filed in the same way," suggested the other pilot, looking as black as a thunder-cloud; because such an act was in his mind the rankest sort of treachery, worthy of only the most degraded man.

"We will find them if there are," replied Tom, resolutely. "And when this thing is known I imagine there'll be a general overhauling of all the machines on the aviation field. One thing is certain, Jack. You were playing in great luck when you suggested that we ask for a day off and then picked out this particular one."

Jack shrugged his shoulders as he replied:

"That's right, Tom."

Nothing could be done just then, with night coming on. Tom talked with several of the attendants at the hangars, and left it to them to go to work with the coming of morning. He even showed them how cunningly the work had been carried out; so they might be on their guard against such a trick from that time forward.

Then the three returned to the villa. Others of the members of the escadrille were in the car with the trio, so the talk was general, experiences of the day's happenings being narrated, all told in a careless fashion, as if those young aviators considered all such risks as part of the ordinary routine of business.

Later on the news concerning Jack's singular warning, and what came of it went the rounds. He was asked to show the brief note many times; but in answer to the questions that came pouring in upon him, Jack could not say more than he had already said with regard to his suspicions concerning the probable writer of the message.

That night Tom and Jack preferred the quiet

of their own apartment to the general sitting-room, where the tired pilots gathered to smoke, talk, play games, sing, and give their opinions on every topic imaginable, including scraps of news received in late letters from home towns across the sea.

"Do you know, Tom," Jack said unexpectedly, "I'd give something to know where Bessie Gleason is just at this time. It's strange how often I think about that young girl. It's just as if something that people call intuition told me she might be in serious trouble through that hard-looking guardian of hers, Carl Potzfeldt."

Tom smiled.

Bessie Gleason was a very pretty and winsome girl of about twelve years of age, with whom Jack in particular had been quite "chummy" on the voyage across the Atlantic, and through the submarine zone, as related in "Air Service Boys Flying for France." The last he had seen of her was when she waved her hand to him when leaving the steamer at its English port. Her stern guardian had contracted a violent dislike for Jack, so that the two had latterly been compelled to meet only in secret for little confidential chats.

"Oh, you've taken to imagining all sorts of terrible things in connection with pretty Bessie and her cruel guardian. He claimed to be a

Swiss, or a native of Alsace-Lorraine, which was it, Jack?"

"Uh-huh," murmured Jack Parmly, his thoughts just then far away from Tom and his question, though fixed on Carl Potzfeldt and his young ward.

Bessie Gleason was a little American girl, a child of moods, fairylike in appearance and of a maturity of manner that invariably attracted those with whom she came in contact.

Her mother had been lost at sea, and by Mrs. Gleason's will the girl and her property were left in Potzfeldt's care. Mr. Potzfeldt was taking her to Europe, and on the steamship she and Jack Parmly had been friends, and as Potzfeldt's actions were suspicious and, moreover, the girl did not seem happy with him Jack had been troubled about her.

"I'm afraid you think too much about Bessie and her troubles, Jack; and get yourself worked up about things that may never happen to her," Tom went on after a pause.

"I knew you'd say that, Tom," the other told him reproachfully. "But I'm not blaming you for it. However, there are several things Bessie told me that I haven't mentioned to you before; and they help to make me feel anxious about her happiness. She's a queer girl, you know, and intensely patriotic."

"Yes, I noticed that, even if you did monopolize most of her time," chuckled Tom.

"How she does hate the Germans, though! And that's what will get her into trouble I'm afraid, if she and her guardian have managed to get through the lines in any way, and back to his home town, wherever that may be."

"Why should she feel so bitter toward the Kaiser and his people, Jack?"

"I'll tell you. Her mother was drowned. She was aboard the *Lusitania*, and was never seen after the sinking. Mr. Potzfeldt was there too, it seems, but couldn't save Mrs. Gleason, he claims, though he tried in every way to do so. She was a distant relative of his, you remember."

"Then if Bessie knows about her mother's death," Tom went on to say, "I don't wonder she feels that way toward everything German. I'd hate the entire race if my mother had been murdered, as those women and children were, when that torpedo was launched against the great passenger steamer without any warning."

"She told me she felt heart-broken because she was far too young to do anything to assist in the drive against the central empires. You see, Bessie has great hopes of some day growing tall enough to become a war nurse. She is deeply interested in the Red Cross; and Tom, would you believe it, the midget practices regular United States Army standing exercises in the hope of hastening her growth."

"I honor the little girl for her ambition," Tom said. "But I'm inclined to think this war will be long past before she has grown to a suitable size to enlist among the nurses of the Paris hospitals. And if that Carl Potzfeldt entertains the sentiments we suspected him of, and is secretly in sympathy with the Huns, although passing for a neutral, her task will be rendered doubly hard."

"That's what makes me feel bad every time I get to thinking of Bessie. If only we could chance to run across them again I'd like to engineer some scheme by which she could be taken away from her guardian. For instance, if only it could be proved that Potzfeldt was in the pay of the German Government, don't you see he could be stood up against a wall, and fixed; and then some one would be found able and willing to take care of the girl."

Tom laughed again.

"How nicely you make your arrangements, Jack! Very pleasant outlook for poor Mr. Potzfeldt, I should say. Why, you hustle him off this earth just as if he didn't matter thirty cents."

LOOKING BACKWARD 51

"It isn't because I'm heartless," expostulated the other hurriedly. "But I'm sure that dark-faced man is a bad egg. We suspected him of being hand-in-glove with Adolph Tuessig, the man who stole your father's invention, and who we knew was a hired German spy over in America. And from little hints Bessie dropped once in a while I am certain he doesn't treat her well."

"Still, we can't do the least thing about it, Jack. If fortune should ever bring us in contact with that pair again, why then we could perhaps think up some sort of scheme to help Bessie. Now, I've got something important to tell you."

"Something the captain must have said when he was chatting with you in the mess-room immediately after supper, I guess. At the time I thought he might be asking you about our adventures of to-day, but then I noticed that he was doing pretty much all the talking. What is on the carpet for us now?"

"We're going to be given our chance at last, Jack!"

"Do you mean to fly with the fighting escadrille, and meet German pilots in a life and death battle up among the clouds?" asked Jack, in a voice that had a tinge of awe about it; for he had often dreamed of such honors coming to him; but the realization still seemed afar off.

"That is what we are promised," his chum assured him. "Of course our education is not yet complete; but we have shown such progress that, as there is need of additional pilots able to meet the Fokker planes while a raid is in progress, we are to be given a showing."

"I'll not sleep much to-night for thinking of it," declared Jack.

CHAPTER VII

THE GREAT DAY ARRIVES

By the time the pilots of the American escadrille began to assemble on the field where the airplane hangars were clustered, (these being more or less camouflaged by means of paint cleverly applied to represent the earth,) the news concerning the air service boys' narrow escape had become generally known.

Great was the indignation expressed by all. Up to this time there had appeared to be considerable honor exhibited among the flying men on both sides. In fact many curious little courtesies had been exchanged that seemed to put the aviation service on a plane of its own.

One thing was certain. After that there would be no taking things for granted. Each pilot meant to satisfy himself as best he could that his plane was in perfect order before risking his life in the upper currents.

Jack was besieged for a full account of the matter. He, being an obliging person, gladly told everything he knew. Naturally the mystery attached to the discovery of the message of warning tied to the poor little partly collapsed child's balloon aroused considerable curiosity and speculation among the aviators.

The way some of them pumped Jack made him laugh; but he assured them he was just about as "deep in the mud as they were in the mire."

"I've told you all about the woman named Mrs. Neumann," he repeated for the tenth time. "And she's the only one I can think of who would be apt to care a cent whether Jack Parmly happened to be alive or dead. If anybody can give a better guess I'd like to hear it."

They did considerable "guessing," but after all it became the consensus of opinion that the grateful Mrs. Neumann was responsible. And so finally they let it go at that; for the day had begun, and there was an abundance of work to be accomplished before the sun set again.

"But this is certain," said one of the leading flyers of the escadrille, seriously; "if the Boches mean to stop playing fair it's bound to demoralize the service. Up to now there's been an unwritten set of rules to the game, which both sides have lived up to. I shall hate to see them discarded, and brutal methods put in their place."

Others were of the opinion that there might have been something personal connected with the attempt to kill Jack, through that shabby trick.

THE GREAT DAY ARRIVES 55

The German spy might have had a private grievance against the youth, they said, which he meant to pay off in his own dastardly way.

No matter which turned out to be the truth, it was not pleasant for Jack to believe he had become an object of hatred to some mysterious prowler, and that possibly other secret attempts on his life might be made from time to time.

That day passed, and another followed. There did not seem to be much stirring on either side of the line; but such a lull frequently proved the precursor of some gigantic battle, for which the armies were preparing.

Of course, when the wind and weather permitted, there was always plenty of excitement among the airplane escadrilles. All manner of little expeditions were organized and carried out.

Now it was an attempt to get above that string of "sausage" balloons used for observation purposes only, so that a few well-dropped bombs might play havoc among them.

As these were always defended by a force of fighting planes hovering above, all primed to give battle on the slightest provocation, the result of these forays was that a number of hotly-contested fights were "pulled off" high in air.

One pilot brought down another enemy, and

increased his score a peg, always a matter of pride with a pilot of a fighting plane. And another of the escadrille had the honor of getting above those observation balloons before a couple of them could be hastily pulled down.

Two of his companions engaged the defending Teuton pilots, and fended them off purposely, in order to permit the raid. The selected man swooped down like a hawk, passed the Gotha guard, and managed to shoot his bomb downward with unerring aim. One of the balloons was seen to burst into flames, and the second must have met with a like fate, since it was perilously near at the time, though the dense smoke obscured everything.

All these things and more did Tom and Jack witness through their glasses as those two days passed. Tom especially was waiting to have his wish realized with as much calmness as he could summon.

"I think it will come to-night, Jack," he told his chum, on the second afternoon, as they prepared to return to their lodgings.

"Then you believe there's some big move on tap, and that to-morrow a battle will be commenced? And all for the possession of some old ruined fort, perhaps, that is now only a mass of crumpled masonry and debris!"

"You mustn't forget, Jack, it is the famous

THE GREAT DAY ARRIVES 57

name that counts with these romantic Frenchmen. Douaumont and Vaux mean everything to them, even if there is nothing but a great mound of stone, mortar and earth to tell where each fort once stood."

"Yes, I suppose you're right, Tom; and then again I was forgetting that the retaking of a prominent position which the Germans had captured means a heartening of the whole army. I've heard them talking of Mort-Homme, and Hill Three Hundred and Four, as if those were the most precious bits of territory in all France."

"These are sometimes strategic points, you know, keys to a further advance. But there comes the captain now, and he's got his eye on us, as sure as you live!" ejaculated Tom, giving a little start, and turning a shade paler than usual, owing to the excess of his emotions, and the anticipation of hearing pleasant news.

The leader of the Lafayette Escadrille smiled as he drew near. He waited until he could speak without being overheard, for it was not always wise to shout aloud when dealing with matters in which the High Command had a deep interest, such as a pending advance movement.

"It is to-morrow, Raymond," he said quietly, yet with a twinkle in his eye.

He had taken a great liking to these daring

lads who had already made such strides toward the goal of becoming "aces" in time, granting that they lived through the risky period of their apprenticeship.

"Both?" gasped Jack eagerly.

The head pilot shook his head in the negative.

"Sorry to disappoint you, Parmly, but you'll have to wait a bit longer," he announced, whereat the other's face fell again, though he gulped, and tried to appear content. "There are several things you must correct before you can expect to take such chances. We are short a fighting pilot for to-morrow, and I thought it was time we gave Raymond his initiation."

Then as he walked alongside the chums he entered into a minute description of the duties that would devolve upon Tom in his first time up to serve as a guardian to the heavier planes acting as "fire-control." and scouts, or "eyes of the army."

"Of course you are only to butt in if we are outnumbered," the leader explained in conclusion. "The experienced and able fliers must take care of such of the enemy as venture to attack our big machines. Some of these Boches will be their best men, with records of a dozen or two machines to their credit. It would be little short of suicide to send a novice up against them, you understand."

THE GREAT DAY ARRIVES 59

Tom was ambitious, and would of course be delighted to prove his metal when opposed by a famous "ace;" whose name and reputation had long made him a terror to the French and British airmen. Nevertheless he recognized the wisdom of what the captain was telling him, and promised to restrain his eagerness until given the prearranged signal that his chance had come.

It made Tom feel proud to know he had won the good opinion of such a brave man as the captain, as well as the friendship of those other gallant souls composing the American squadron of aviators fighting for France.

"Still," he said to Jack later on, when they were together in their room getting into their ordinary street clothes, "it made me feel a bit cheap when he spoke of my being pitted against just an *ordinary* pilot, some fresh hand as anxious as we are to achieve a reputation. At the same time that's what we must seem to these veterans of scores of air combats, all of whom have met with the most thrilling adventures again and again."

Jack managed to hide his bitter disappointment. He realized that he would never be in the same class as his more brilliant chum. Tom was fitted for becoming an expert in the line he had chosen for his calling. On the other hand Jack began to believe that he was a little too slow-witted ever to make a shining success as a fighting aviator, where skill must be backed by astonishing quickness of mind and body, as well as *something else* within the heart that is an inherited birthright.

"Anyhow," he consoled himself by saying, not aloud, but softly, "I can be the pilot of a bombing machine, and perhaps in time they'll give me charge of a plane used as fire-control during the battle. That is as far up the pole as I ought to aspire to climb. These chaps in the Lafayette are one and all picked men, the very cream of the entire service."

CHAPTER VIII

OVER THE ENEMY'S LINES

"I SAY, Tom, it looks like a poor day for flying I'm afraid," Jack called out in the chill of the early dawn the next morning, he having been the first to get out of bed and step over to the window of their sleeping room.

It was of course in the villa placed at the disposal of the escadrille, many miles back of the first line of trenches.

Tom, however, did not bother his head about the weather to any appreciable extent.

"It's likely to turn out a fair day for work," he told his chum, in his cheery way, as he followed Jack to the window. "You know that's happened lots of times. So far we've been lucky enough not to get caught in a storm while aloft. Yes, I can already see that there isn't going to be a stiff breeze; and what would a sprinkle of rain amount to?"

"I suppose the thing has to be pulled off, no matter what the weather is," mused Jack, as he proceeded to dress, since breakfast had been ordered at an unusually early hour that morning.

"Well, the High Command has made all

arrangements for a big time. You know what that means, when tens of thousands of poilus have to be transferred during the darkness of night, so that the enemy pilots can't glimpse the movement and give warning? So, unless the skies fall, we are bound to get busy this morning."

The air service boys were soon at the hangars, where an animated scene was taking place. Any one could see that something unusual was about to take place, because of the numbers of men rushing this way and that, while motors were popping and machine-guns being tried out so as to be certain they were in prime condition for service. Scores of mechanicians, chauffeurs, observers, as well as other helpers, went about their work of getting "ready for business."

The air fighters were dressed in their fur-lined union suits, with fur overcoats, gloves, and caps; for they would soon be soaring to great heights, where the atmosphere was almost Arctic in its intensity.

They were examining their automatic pistols, seeing that their airplane compasses, speed indicators, special airplane clocks, mounted on wire springs, and altitude barometers were in their proper places and in working order. Their very lives might depend on a little thing, and no one could afford to neglect even trifles.

Every few minutes one of the planes would roll over the surface of the level ground in front of the long line of hangars. Then, when sufficient momentum had been attained, it would commence to climb swiftly upward. Soon the machine would get into spirals like a winding staircase, and mount toward an altitude of perhaps four thousand feet, there to await the coming of companion craft before heading toward the battleground, far distant.

Jack squeezed the hand of his chum, and gave him one last look. There was no need of words to tell the deep feelings that gripped his loyal heart; indeed, Jack was utterly unable to utter a single sentence.

Then Tom was off.

He made the ascent with his customary brilliancy, which had won him the admiration of the entire escadrille. The air seemed to be filled with various types of planes. Some were already moving off toward the front, from which came the roar of battle, showing that already the action had begun by an intense bombardment of a portion of the German trenches which the French longed to retake.

Tom spent some little time "knocking around" while awaiting the coming of those members of the Lafayette Escadrille who were the last to leave the ground.

What is twenty or even thirty miles to a pilot in a speedy Neiuport capable of going two miles a minute when pressed? They could be over the lines in a very brief time after leaving the aviation camp.

Tom looked at the scene below him, which was spread out like a gigantic map. He never wearied of observing it when simply "loafing" up in the air, as at present. The sun was fairly above the eastern horizon, though clouds drifted along in scattered masses, and it was as yet impossible to tell what the day might bring forth.

Then the last of the squadron arrived, and the signal was given to start for the front. Away they went with a whirr and a roar, seven strong. They overtook a number of clumsy two-seaters on the way, observation planes, bombing machines, or it might be those included in the "fire-control" units going to relieve some of their kind already doing their appointed bit in the battle.

Tom looked far beyond. He could see great oceans of smoke arising that told of innumerable high explosives bursting, and enormous guns being discharged. Both sides seemed hard at work, though the French were certainly sending ten shells to one that came from the forces of the Crown Prince. This told plainly enough which army expected to do the attacking that day.

And yet while all this wonderful panorama of war was spread beneath them, the seven pilots moving onward in wild-geese formation, with the captain at the head of the V, they heard nothing of the tumult raging. In their muffled ears sounded only the loud whirr of the propellers, and the deafening explosions of the engines. It was almost as noisy as a boiler shop in full blast.

The fire-control planes were already sending back their signals, the observer aboard intently following the course of each monster shell to note exactly where it landed, and then communicating with the gunners, so they might correct their faults and make each missile count.

German pilots were in the air also, sometimes in swarms. Theirs was the task to attack these heavier machines and try to cripple or destroy them.

Of course each one of these machines of the French "relage," or fire-control, was armed with a quick-firing gun; and there was an observer aboard, as well as a deft pilot. They carried such a large assortment of material, consisting among other things of a complete wireless outfit, that they had to be built with unusually large wings.

This makes them slow to answer to the call of the pilot; and when attacked by the more nimble Fokkers they have a hard time to keep from being shot down. That is why a number of the Nieuports with well known "aces" in charge, must always be hovering over the fire controls, ready to fly to their assistance in case they are attacked.

"Things are surely beginning to happen," murmured Tom. "The Boches seem to be in an unusually fierce and aggressive humor on this particular morning."

The youth was right in this. The Germans had been thrown out of numerous hard-won positions lately, and this gave them cause for feeling bitterly toward the French.

By the time the American unit reached the field of battle, several furious combats had already taken place with disastrous results. Two of the enemy machines had been sent down, one of them in flames, after the pilot had fallen at his post, fairly riddled by the gunfire of the Frenchman. A birdman had also paid the great debt on the side of Petain's men. As the score was two against one there seemed no cause for depression.

The Americans would not be kept out of the fight for long. No sooner were three adventurous Teuton pilots seen climbing up to attack the big fire control machine when Tom's companions dropped down from the "ceiling" to engage them.

Tom watched everything as though photographing the thrilling happenings on his brain forever. He had a greater interest in these things than at any previous period of his life, for was he not also hovering over that observation Caudron, upon which the movements of the advancing French troops depended? At any minute might he not receive the signal from the captain to attack some fresh Boche, who had climbed high above the battle lines to join the general scrimmage, or else "get" the big French machine while its defenders had their hands full with his comrades?

Had Tom been able to use his binoculars just then, which was out of the question of course, and look back to where the monster French guns were firing, he might have noticed various white sheets spread out in fantastic patterns on the ground, the picture varying every little while.

These were used to "talk" with the observer who was sending those messages from the fire-control plane, telling the gunners just how many metres their fire was short, long, to the right, or to the left of their intended objective.

Then again information was being sent by

another observer to the advancing infantry, warning them of perils that lay in their way, which might have cost them great and grievous losses if they remained unknown until the German trap was sprung.

The morning was advancing. Tom had seen his comrades chase off several flocks of enemy aircraft that endeavored to interrupt the deadly work of the observers. As yet his anticipated chance had not come. He was beginning to feel impatient. Could it be that he must stay there almost up among the clouds, and only be a "looker-on?"

How eagerly did his heart throb with renewed hope each time he discovered signs of another attempt on the part of the enemy pilots to engineer a raid that might check this observation work. They knew what it was doing to advance the cause of the battling French; and that, as often proved to be the case, the airplanes were again the "vigilant eyes of the army."

It was well along in the morning when Tom Raymond's time came. The fighting below had been going on for some time, and from fugitive glimpses Tom snatched every now and then as he looked down, he had reason to believe things were moving successfully for the assailants. At least the French troops occupied a long line of trenches where the Boches had been in possession at the close of the previous day.

Yes, there was another burst of ambitious fliers rising to take a chance. The fact that already seven of their men had been dropped, several with their planes ablaze, did not deter them; for those German airmen had often proved their courage and were known as stubborn fighters.

Soon another battle below the clouds was in progress. Besides Tom, there were now only three of the Americans in the air, the remainder having been driven down, some in trouble of some kind, others to replenish their supplies. And there were *four* enemy planes, Tom noticed, even as he watched the machine of the captain and received the signal to attack the latest arrival in the enemy squadron.

CHAPTER IX

WINNING HIS SPURS

"AT LAST!"

Those were the expressive words that broke from Tom Raymond's lips when he saw the commander give him the long-anticipated signal. Tom had already discovered his intended antagonist. A fourth plane was coming up quickly. It had held back to await the chance that would be offered when the three defenders of the fire-control machine were hotly engaged with the trio of skillful Boche pilots.

The game was very apparent. It was likewise exceedingly old. The French commander was too experienced an aviator to be so easily caught. That was why he had signaled to Tom to take care of the fourth and last German airman, and guard the important observation plane.

Tom started down with a rush, just as a hungry hawk might swoop upon a pigeon it had marked for its intended pray.

"I've got to make good!" the young aviator told himself. "I've got to make good!"

The German pilot saw him coming. He had more than half expected to be interfered with in his designs; but it would please him first of all to riddle this ambitious young airman, and his Nieuport, and then to accomplish his main purpose.

Now the two were so close that Tom could plainly see the black Maltese crosses on the wings of the Teuton plane as it tilted in climbing. Already had the other opened fire on him, for as his motor was silent during his first long dive Tom could catch the tut-tut-tut of the rapidly exploding mitrailleuse.

Somehow this did not unnerve him in the least, as he had feared it might. Even when he realized that the missiles were cutting holes through the wings a few feet away he did not grow uneasy. The spirit of battle had gripped Tom. He was now attaining what had seemed to be the height of his ambition. He was trying out his mettle against one of the enemy pilots, a man with considerable more experience than himself, and therefore well fitted to spur him on to do his level best.

He could see the pilot crouched in his place, and working his gun with one hand while he managed some controls of his fleeting machine with the other, for there was only one man aboard, though German machines usually hold two. Long practice had made him an adept at this sort of thing, it seemed.

But then Tom had been taught the same clever trick down at the French school of aviation at Pau, and over on the lake at Casso. He was now about to show whether he had learned his lesson to advantage. It was French ways pitted against those of the German school.

Tom tried to aim directly at the foeman as he rushed toward him. Then he pressed the release hard, and instantly the rapid-fire gun commenced its staccato barking, as it spit out the bullets.

Crack! crack! crack! crack!

Thus the two rivals, rushing at each other like opposing birds of enormous size, passed and dived, as though ducking to avoid the hot fire. Tom looked back, hoping to discover the enemy winged and dropping out of the fight. Nothing of the kind occurred; but on the contrary his antagonist was sailing on, apparently untouched, at least in any vital point.

That meant it must all be tried over again. The second round in the air duel was about to open. It was impossible to predict what the outcome might be, but at any rate Tom felt renewed courage and confidence.

If he had passed through one siege unscathed he believed he could show considerable improvement the next time. Already had he learned how he might avoid several little errors of judgment, not much in themselves possibly; but which tended to interfere with his doing the one thing necessary—firing point blank into the muffled face of the German pilot.

WINNING HIS SPURS 73

Once more were they rushing headlong toward each other. Tom was steadier now, and more alert. He had his plan of campaign mapped out clearly in his mind. He had moreover noticed a weak point about the other's method of attack, of which he intended to take advantage.

The other three Americans were just as hotly engaged not far away; but it was a case of every man for himself. Tom counted on receiving no assistance. Indeed, while that feeling of confidence pulsed through his veins he would have scorned to call for help, or even to allow it, if he could prevent such a thing.

Again the guns opened fire as the two foes advanced with savage fury. Such a battle in the clouds is on a plane that almost beggars description. Nothing resembling it has ever been known before in all the annals of history until the present world war broke out, and the airplane was perfected as it stands to-day.

This attack was even more tumultuous than the first had been. The planes tried dodging, and several tricks were brought to bear on either side; for it seems that every pilot has his pet theories as to how best to catch an opponent napping. Everything is fair, once the battle royal has started and German wit is matched against American, or French.

Again did they pass each other for a sudden

dip. Each feared to be caught in a condition that would not permit of defense. They looked for all the world like a couple of agile boxers engaged in a contest, in which foot-work counted almost as much as that of the fists.

Around and around they flew, coming back to the attack a third, and even a fourth time. Tom was beginning to grow impatient. Try as he could, he did not seem able to bring the other down, though he was almost sure he had poked his rapid-fire gun straight for the German's face, and when only a comparatively short distance away.

"I've got to get him!" he muttered. "Or else he'll get me!"

He wondered whether there could be anything in what he had heard one old aviator say, to the effect that he firmly believed some of those Germans must be wearing armor or suits of mail, since he had poured streams of missiles straight at them, and without the least appreciable effect.

The German was getting a bit reckless. No doubt he had anticipated an easy victory over the other, whom he must have guessed was something of a beginner at this sort of aerial combat. Tom's agility in avoiding punishment annoyed him; likewise the way the bullets splashed around him had a disconcerting effect on his mind.

This was the fifth dash, and it seemed as though the time had come when one or the other should win the contest. They were growing more and more desperate now; the fire of the battle had gone to their heads, and each must have made up his mind to finish the fight then and there, judging from the way they headed straight toward one another. At any rate Tom had determined that he must win, and win without delay.

Bang!

Tom realized suddenly that he had been struck, for he felt a sudden acute twinge. He neither knew nor cared how serious the injury might be, so long as it did not incapacitate him from serving his machine. And, best of all, thus far no missile from that popping mitrailleuse of the German had done serious damage to the vitals of his plane.

Let the bullets cut holes all they pleased through the linen of the wings; there would be no splitting, as happens in the case of cotton or other fabrics; and such tiny apertures do not count for much in retarding the upholding power of a plane.

Another dash, and this time Tom felt absolutely certain he had made a hit. It seemed to him he must have fairly riddled the other pilot, so close was he when he poured all that torrent of lead aboard his craft.

They rushed past one another, but Tom took the earliest possible opportunity to redress, and look back at his foe. A thrill ran through his entire being as he discovered that the other was in trouble. The Fokker was descending in erratic spirals, evidently out of control. Man or machine, perhaps both, had come within the deadly line of fire, and the fight was over.

Turning, Tom watched the enemy plane go down. He had a queer, choking sensation in his throat. Every novice probably feels that when he watches his first rival heading earthward, with a mile or more to fall before he strikes. Still, Tom grimly held his feelings in check. A successful air pilot, especially when he manages a fighting craft, can not let sentiment get the better of his combative spirit. It is a fair test of skill and endurance, and as a rule the better man wins the game. And war must always be an exhibition of cruelty in that human lives are the stake played for.

Nevertheless Tom was secretly glad to discover that the plane was being fairly well guided to earth, showing that the German pilot, though he had lost his fight, could not have been killed outright, or even mortally wounded.

Tom now found a chance to look around, and note what was going on. It was just then that one of the leading American aviators drove at his antagonist in a series of zigzag spins that must have bewildered the German, he never having run up against such tactics before.

The consequence was the enemy met defeat. Tom knew what was going to happen as soon as he saw the chief star of the Lafayette Escadrille start his favorite attack. And ten seconds afterwards a second Teuton plane was whirling around aimlessly and falling. It turned in its flight so that its white belly showed plainly just as a fish will in its death throes.

But the pilot was game to the finish, and managed in some wonderful fashion to swing his damaged craft around again, so that when it landed with a crash it fell bottom-down, and the motor did not come on top of him.

Later on Tom learned that the man was badly injured, and made a prisoner. Eventually he pulled through, though it was reported he would never be fit for flying again, even if he gained his freedom.

The other two Germans had retreated, deeming the Americans too strong for them. And Tom hoped it would be some time before others could muster up sufficient courage to go aloft, to pit their machines with those of the members of the Lafayette Escadrille.

CHAPTER X

AFTER THE BATTLE

During all this turmoil the fire-control plane pilot had kept his machine at work. While the fighting guard engaged the German, the observer aboard the larger craft continued to send his signals to the batteries far in the rear of the French advanced lines; and through the successful working of the undertaking a number of heavy Teuton guns had already been silenced.

Tom now found time to look down, using his glasses for the purpose, since the air in their immediate vicinity was clear of enemy planes. He could see something of the battle, though so much smoke lay above the battleground that it was only when this lifted temporarily that an occasional fugitive glimpse could be obtained of the earth.

The French were undoubtedly pushing the Germans well out of their advance trenches. They had already gone forward far enough to redeem a fairly wide stretch of territory that had been taken from them at the time the forces of the Crown Prince made their forward drive, at the cost of more than a hundred thousand men.

AFTER THE BATTLE

Tom now felt another twinge in his shoulder. On looking into the matter he discovered, as he suspected, that he had been wounded. Blood was showing on his thick fur-lined coat.

Just then a plane approached him. Tom recognized the mark on the side, and knew the muffled figure seated in the machine was the commander of the escadrille. He was coming to ascertain whether the novice had drawn out of his first combat entirely unscathed.

He had, in truth, cast many an anxious, fleeting look toward the pair while Tom was "doing his bit" for France; for after discovering that the German was an experienced pilot, and a man to be feared, the captain would gladly have flown to the relief of Tom only that he had his hands full with the Teuton he had attacked.

He made motions as he approached at reduced speed. Tom could not hear a sound save the loud beat of his own motor, but he knew what the other was asking.

So he touched his left shoulder with his finger, and held that up to show that it was reddened. Then the Captain made a quick motion that was meant for a command. Tom was to go down. There was no necessity for his remaining aloft longer, now that another had arrived to relieve him from the post of duty. He ought to call it a day's work, and have his shoulder attended to.

Regretfully Tom obeyed. His fighting spirit was aroused, and he would gladly have accepted a second challenge to combat, had the opportunity come. He nodded his head to show he understood, and then started back toward the French lines.

All this time shrapnel had been bursting here, there and everywhere underneath them; but no one paid much attention to the shower. Indeed, shrapnel does not account for as many hostile planes as might be imagined; since each looks like a fly when ten thousand feet high, and the surrounding space is so vast.

So Tom swung past the advance French lines, just as they were making another forward movement. He could glimpse long lines of poilus streaming over the shell-hole pitted terrain like ants in army array. Tom would have been pleased to hover above them for a while, and watch how those furious fighters rushed the Boches out of their second line trenches, as though nothing could stay their push.

Beyond the French barrage fire was falling like a curtain. Tom could tell this from the constant line of explosions that took place. The

AFTER THE BATTLE

Germans in the second trenches would have no chance of going back through that deadly hailstorm of shells; they must either die at their posts, or surrender, he saw.

So fifteen minutes later Tom dropped to the field, ran his plane up close to the hangar, and then as a figure dashed wildly toward him, started to climb wearily from his seat.

Of course it was Jack. He was wild with delight, and was swinging his cap above his head with all the animation of a schoolboy.

"Oh! to think that I saw it all, Tom!" was what he cried, as he seized the hand of his chum, and squeezed it fiercely, almost crying in his excitement.

"You did!" exclaimed the other. "How did that happen, when I had the glasses aloft with me?"

"Oh, I borrowed a pair from an obliging French officer. When he understood that you were my chum, and that it was your first trial at combat in the air, he gladly accommodated me. They are willing to do almost anything for us Americans. My heart was up in my throat every time you rushed at that terrible Boche pilot!"

"But how could you pick me out at that distance?" demanded Tom incredulously, for it seemed almost unbelievable.

"I guessed that our captain would have you hold back when he and the other two started to meet the rising Germans," said Jack. "You see, I was wise enough to believe he would want you to butt in only in case a fourth Boche came along. And when that happened I knew your chance had come."

"It was pretty exciting while it lasted," remarked Tom grimly.

They were soon on the road to the villa, going in one of the cars used to take the pilots when going to and returning from work. There was a surgeon at hand, and an examination of Tom's hurt was made. It proved to be a small matter, though it had bled quite freely.

"You must take a few days' rest, young M'sieu," the army surgeon told the young aviator after he had dressed the wound. "It was a narrow escape, I assure you. Three inches further down, and I would not like to have answered for your life. But evidently France had further need of your excellent services. I salute you, M'sieu Raymond, you have this day done your duty well, and won your spurs."

The air service boys could not remain quietly at the villa while all that furor was going on. They wished to be at the hangars, to greet those who returned, and give the pilots who

AFTER THE BATTLE

were sallying forth a last word of encouragement.

It was a long day, and full of thrilling happenings. Other battles in the air occurred along the extended front, and not all of them wound up in victories for the Allied forces. Some distinguished Teuton "aces" were flying on that occasion who would not be denied their toll. But the Lafayette Escadrille lost none of its members, Tom and Jack were glad to learn.

Night finally set its pall over the field where all day long the hostile armies had fought and bled. The French were grimly holding their seized terrain, and hurling the Germans back again and again. The serried ranks had pushed forward up to within an hour of sunset; then, apparently realizing that it was a hopeless task, the Teuton High Command had given the order to withdraw.

On the following day the battle was not resumed. The French had their hands full in strengthening and fortifying their new positions, while the Germans must have been so severely punished and "shot to pieces" that they needed time to effect the reorganization of their various battalions and regiments.

So several days passed, and nothing out of the ordinary happened, at least in connection with the two chums. Tom's slight wound was healing fast, and he was told by the army surgeon that it would be quite safe for him to go up again at any time now, a fact that pleased the young aviator immensely.

"I'm going to make a record for myself," he told his chum.

"You're the fellow to do it," answered Jack. "Wish I was in your shoes."

CHAPTER XI

A SHOW ON THE FRONT

WHILE the fighting on the Verdun front was furious at times, with prolonged spasms when the Germans seemed determined to recover the territory they had lost to the French, there were also periods of almost total calm.

During these quiet periods the members of the American escadrille were sometimes hard pushed for ways in which to pass the time away, and amuse themselves. Inaction fretted most of them, since they were endowed with that restless spirit which seems to be the inherent trait of most Americans.

Many were the expedients tried by means of which some amusement might be extracted from life. Their daily business was so exciting that these slumps left the aviators nervous and unhappy. It was like the sailor who, bowling along under full pressure of canvas for weeks, in the old days of the sailing vessel, suddenly found himself in the "doldrums," and becalmed for what might be an indefinite period—it was apt to wear upon a nervous system that demanded work.

Of course the pilots were merry while at meals

and during their loafing periods; but every time one of their number returned from the front and reported the inaction as still continuing, many deep sighs of discontent would arise.

Then a clever thought occurred to some one of the men. Perhaps it was suggested by a happy-go-lucky Irish aviator who was connected with the British air forces, and wore the marks of distinguished service on his arm and cap.

Sergeant Barney McGee had received a month's furlough in order to recover from injuries which he had sustained. Instead of going back to Ireland to spend his enforced vacation, as one might naturally expect him to do, McGee put in the time visiting other parts of the long front between Ypres and Verdun.

After all, there was nothing so very singular about that. Give an old railroad engineer a week off, and presently you will discover him spending the time loafing around the roundhouse, chatting with the other engineers, and investigating things. His whole life being wrapped up in his work his idea of a vacation consists of being free to watch his fellows of the same craft work.

Sergeant McGee was an exceedingly droll chap. He spent a couple of weeks with a French cousin who was also an aviator, and in time came to know the jolly members of the Lafayette Escadrille. He grew to be exceedingly fond of them all, and was in the mess-room nearly every night.

His idea was that they should get up a show to pass these dull evenings away. If the enemy allowed them sufficient time they could even give a public performance, and give the proceeds to the Red Cross.

It took like wild-fire with the Americans, casting about at the time for some way to kill dull care, and make the hours pass more quickly until called to action again.

A survey developed the fact that there were a number in and out of the Lafayette Escadrille who possessed a talent of some kind or other. This one had a violin which he loved to play; and, while not a finished artist, he was able to make real and lovely music by means of his clever bow. Another, it turned out, had a good tenor voice, and knew many of the most popular songs of the day. A third showed a talent for mimicking well known people, particularly Americans of national fame. Several agreed to black up, and give a humorous little minstrel skit that they declared would set the house in a roar.

It was Barney McGee himself who most astonished the Americans, however. At the first rehearsal he appeared before their astonished eyes dressed to imitate a well known and popular moving picture star and he carried out the part in a fashion that caused the wildest excitement. From that moment the success of the show was assured.

They made feverish preparations, for no one could tell just when the period of inaction would come to an end, and every available member of the several fraternizing escadrilles be ordered to rush to the front again, to take his life in his hands, and risk it hourly for the great cause.

Tom and Jack both had parts in the entertainment. Jack made a good "bones" for the minstrels, and he coaxed his chum to don a burnt-cork face for that one evening, and show what he could do as a comedian of parts.

They found a building in Bar-le-Duc that could be used, and which would hold a respectable sized audience. Little preparation was needed save to build a stage and get seating arrangements. Where chairs were not available benches had to take their place. Lights were also provided, and what few accessories they needed, such as curtains and stage scenery, were improvised after a fashion.

In the spirit of fun that prevailed "any old thing went," as Jack expressed it. The makeshifts that came to light when the performers appeared dressed for their various parts were many and startling. They had borrowed or begged anything that promised to answer the purpose from a long-tailed French coat to a lady's highly colored shawl. Wigs had been sent for, and Paris had responded with an assortment that left nothing to be desired.

The members of the two French air squadrons whose headquarters were near by, had entered into the affair with great zest. They blessed the little Irish pilot for his suggestion. And Sergeant Barney McGee was on the jump all day long, displaying all the sterling traits that distinguish able generals and leaders of men.

The time approached when the entertainment was to come off. The performers were sure of a full house, provided no war orders were issued that would interfere with the arrangements.

"Since Fritz has kept quiet for so many dreary days now," one pilot was heard to say on the morning of the entertainment, "let us hope we'll have just one more peaceful evening to reap the reward of all this training. It would break the heart of Sergeant Barney if the order came for every one to buckle down to hard work just when his big show is about to come off."

The weather man proved friendly, for he gave them a splendid day, with the promise of a moonlight night. Besides, the cold had pretty well vanished, and it was really becoming more seasonable, with the sun warming the earth, and the mud drying up to a considerable extent.

When the show opened that night it was to a house jammed to the doors. Even the windows were utilized for seating room; and crowds stood without, unable to gain admittance.

"Some crowd, eh?" remarked Jack, as he watched the airmen, soldiers and others pouring in.

"I should say so!" cried Tom. "I hope we make good."

It was certainly a unique performance, considering the fact that it was given in a camp close to the battle lines; and that at any hour every one of those who were dressed so fancifully and conducted themselves as actors born to the stage, might be called on to mount to the clouds, and perform their dangerous work of fighting for France, perhaps even giving up their lives.

Loud applause greeted every individual act. The violin music drew tears from eyes unused to weeping, because the strains of "Way Down Upon the Suwannee River," "Home, Sweet

A SHOW ON THE FRONT 91

Home," and other loved airs tenderly and beautifully played, as they were, carried the Americans back again to those near and dear, those whom they might never again see on this earth.

The songs were rapturously applauded, and the singers forced to give encore after encore. One youth who played the part of a little maid from school, and sang in a sweet soprano voice, caused the greatest enthusiasm of the evening; but then everything seemed to make a decided hit.

Tom and Jack, as members of the minstrel troupe, did their parts well, though neither professed to be a star of the first magnitude. They certainly enjoyed seeing and hearing the others go through with their appointed tasks. As for Sergeant Barney McGee, he drew the house down every time he appeared on the stage in his quaint dress, and with the famous walk that is the trade-mark of the character whom he represented.

Two-thirds of the entire show was soon carried out. Indeed, the rest was to be more or less a repetition of preceding acts, though the pleased audience seemed eager to sit for another hour, and applaud each turn vigorously and uproariously.

However, it was not fated that the evening

should pass entirely without some interruption. Afterwards the actors, and those who had enjoyed the performance from in front, agreed that they had been exceedingly lucky as it was, and that "half a loaf was much better than no bread at all."

Those whose turns were finished remained, of course, as part of the audience. Some of the black-faced artists lingered in the so-called "wings" to watch what was going on, desirous of getting all the fun possible out of the evening.

It was not a case of "eat, drink, and be merry, for to-morrow we die;" but "have all the happy times you can, fellows, while the going is good, for to-morrow we fight."

Sergeant Barney McGee was on again, and the audience was convulsed with laughter over his ludicrous antics. He appeared to be a born actor and mimic; and had they not known otherwise Tom and Jack could have declared that the comedian who was under contract with an American film company, and doubtless in California making pictures at that moment, had been suddenly transported to the French fighting front to entertain the soldiers.

Suddenly the laughter came to a stop. The building in which the show was being held shook as though a violent thunderclap had rocked the earth. This loud detonation that broke upon their hearing, however, was only too familiar to all those army aviators. They understood its dread meaning.

The enemy had taken this opportunity to send over a squadron of raiding Fokkers to bomb the hangars of the French and American fliers at Bar-le-Duc!

CHAPTER XII

CLOWNS ON THE WING

Boom!

What followed that first heavy detonation was very much like a riot. The audience became frantic under the belief that it meant an attack on the town, and that the missiles would presently drop upon the roofs, working destruction to everything around.

It was the actors, however, who were the most exercised. One and all they understood what it meant to them. Their planes were in danger of being demolished! In some way the Teutons must have learned about the entertainment, and realized that almost every Allied pilot would want to attend it. They rightly guessed that for once the guard about the aviation field and numerous hangars where the dozens upon dozens of planes of every description were housed when not in use, would be unusually light. They had also taken advantage of the bright moonlight to make a bold sally over the French lines and reach this distant point undiscovered.

Boom! boom! boom!

Other crashing sounds announced that the

enemy machines were busily at work. Each pilot pictured the entire camp under bombardment, with the utmost disaster overtaking the airplanes upon which General Petain was depending so much to serve as the "eyes" of his brave army.

There was a general and maddened rush. Every one wanted to get to the camp in the briefest possible space of time. There was no chance for the actors to change their clothes. They were glad enough of an opportunity to snatch up a heavy fur-lined coat, either their own or some other person's. With this to hide their ludicrous attire, and also give some needed warmth once they went aloft, they hastened to find a waiting car, which, when loaded to its capacity, would be sent like mad along the road to the aviation field.

It was one of the most amazing sights imaginable, to see those pilots, many of whom were world famous, thus garbed. It looked as though some asylum of freaks had opened its doors and allowed the inmates to escape to the highways and byeways.

Only one thought possessed them all, which was to get to the hangars in the shortest possible time. When they arrived each anticipated seeking his particular plane. If that chanced to be out of commission, then commandeering any other, it mattered little whose, so long as they were able to go up, and give battle to the audacious Teuton pilots who had raided their camp at Bar-le-Duc.

"We've got to save our machines!" cried Tom. "Come on!"

"Right you are!" responded Jack.

Tom and Jack were with the rest who found some way to crowd aboard one of the waiting cars that were seized upon to carry the pilots to the field. As they went booming furiously along the road they could still hear those frightful explosions ahead, each one accompanied by a flash as of lightning. The reports were almost deafening.

Eager eyes were turned aloft. The moon shone, but it was difficult to make out so small an object as an airplane at a height of a mile or more without the use of searchlights, and even these were not very efficient on such a night.

Still, some of the pilots believed they could see several enemy planes swooping over at a lower level, possibly, they thought, on the lookout for the procession of cars bearing the aroused Allied aviators to the hangars.

Bang!

A bomb fell not fifty feet away from the car in which the two chums were seated. One of

CLOWNS ON THE WING

their companions received a trifling wound from the effect of the explosion of the TNT contents of the bomb, said to be the most powerful known for such uses, and handled by the engineers of all the armies, under different names.

If the design of the Boche who swooped down for the purpose of waylaying the cars carrying the French and American airmen was to rob the Allies of the services of a dozen eminent pilots all at once, it failed in execution.

At last the aviators arrived on the scene. It was lively enough, with bombs still bursting here and there. Already considerable damage had been done to some of the hangars.

The Allied pilots were "mad all the way through" at having been caught napping by the foe. They paid no attention to the danger that still hung over their heads, with the enemy's supply of explosives as yet unexhausted. While the dreadful detonations continued, sometimes exceedingly close by, the various pilots seized upon such mechanicians as they could.

One by one the planes rolled along the field and began to climb upward by way of the usual spiral staircase route, to give battle to the enemy, regardless of any superiority in numbers.

Jack was dismayed to discover that his plane was badly wrecked by one of the explosions. Indeed, it was afterwards found that he had to have a new machine, since the repairs necessary to put the old one into service again were too complicated to be done at the front.

Tom was more fortunate. His hangar had also suffered to some extent, but so far as could be seen in a hasty examination his plane was not injured in the least.

He too went up, burnt-corked face and all. There were clowns abroad that night who could give Tom many points in the game, so far as comical looks went, and still easily win the stakes. But all else was forgotten under the spur of the moment, save that each man was eager to get in touch with the Boche pilots who had almost spoiled their one great evening.

But no longer were those crashing detonations coming. This told the story only too well. The Germans had either exhausted their supply of bombs, or else they deemed discretion the better part of valor. They had evidently taken their departure before the first Allied pilot got up to the elevation they had been using in their bombardment.

Nothing could be seen of them, though had the Allied pilots been able to use their ears, which was impossible when their own motors

CLOWNS ON THE WING

were making such loud noises, they might have heard, in the distance and to the east, the telltale music of Teuton propellers beating the air in a rush for home ports.

A pursuit was organized, and several planes followed the retreating invaders over the entire distance to the front; but it was of no avail. The enemy planes had had too good a start, and were being pushed for all they were worth to get beyond the danger zone.

There had been several accidents at the Bar-le-Duc field, but none of them fatal. This was not at all surprising, considering the haste shown by the pilots to mount and engage the foemen.

Too, several of the planes besides Jack's had been damaged, a circumstance which brought about disaster before the aviator was able to leave the ground.

As the fliers came back one after another, filled with indignation and disappointed hopes, Jack stalked about, with his black face, yet laughed to see what comical pictures most of his fellow aviators made.

By degrees most of them began to realize that the joke was on them, and joined in greeting with noisy shouts each fresh arrival from above. The damage had not been so very serious after all, since most of the Teuton bombs had either failed to explode when aimed true, or else only dug enormous craters in the ground where it did not matter, sometimes even a quarter of a mile away from the hangars. Jack's machine, it was found, was the only one badly damaged.

From that time there was one subject on which American and French pilots were agreed. They must certainly repay their enemy rivals for this visitation. The honors could not continue to be all on one side.

So from that hour every Allied pilot who went far back of the German lines used his glasses diligently, in the endeavor to locate the secret aviation field of the Boche. This would naturally be camouflaged in the customary fashion, at which the Teutons had become almost as proficient as the French; but trust an airman to spy out the lodging place of his kind.

Step by step they learned which direction the enemy planes took in coming to the front, and retiring when through for the day. Thus in good time the hiding place was found. Great was the delight of the whole Lafayette Escadrille when this confidential news was passed about. And, later on, a party of Allied aviators paid a night visit to the German camp, and dropped several tons of high explosives from bombing planes, that were heavily guarded by the fighting Nieuports.

They had reason to believe from what they themselves saw, as well as through a secret report received from a French spy, that their aim had been remarkably fine; and that many times the amount of damage the Germans had done at Bar-le-Duc had been carried out on the reprisal sally.

After that it seemed as though the slate had been wiped clean. Their honor had been fully purged of the stain that had rested on it ever since that dreadful night when they were caught off their guard.

It turned out that the enemy had meant to start an action on the following day, and it had been hoped that the squadron of airmen might so cripple the French service that the advantage would be all on the side of the assailants.

Something happened, however, to balk the plans of the Crown Prince. Perhaps he had a reprimand from his august father and emperor for so recklessly sacrificing such vast numbers of his men in a fruitless assault against the stone-wall defensive of the French army. It may also have been something else that called the attack off, but at any rate it failed of accomplishment.

The stagnation along the front continued; but all this while General Petain was making quiet though effective preparations, in order some day to strike a staggering blow, such as the French had before given, which would take the enemy by surprise, and push him still further back.

Jack was fretting because thus far he had seen so little of real action. Since his Nieuport had been sent away, and another had as yet failed to arrive for his use, he often bewailed his ill-luck. He even assured his chum the "green mould would be growing all over his person if something didn't soon come to pass to break the terrible monotony."

But every lane, however long, must have its turning; and Jack's hour struck at last.

CHAPTER XIII

MORE WORK IN PROSPECT

"Tom, sit down here on this bench, won't you? I want to have a little talk with you about some things that have bothered me a whole lot lately," said Jack, some days after the exciting experiences narrated in the two preceding chapters.

"I can give a pretty good guess what they are, Jack, since I see you staring hard at the slip of paper found attached to the toy balloon which drifted over our lines from somewhere back of the German front."

"Yes; I own up I do sit and look at that paper, Tom. If it could only talk I'd know who penned that warning, and my curiosity'd be satisfied for one thing. But try as hard as I may, I can't be certain whether it was Mrs. Neumann, or somebody else. But I wanted to speak to you about Bessie just now."

"What about her, Jack?" asked Tom, knowing how much his chum was concerned over the unknown fate of the pretty young girl they had met on the Atlantic liner, and who was apparently anything but happy in the charge of her legally appointed guardian, Carl Potzfeldt.

"There are several things she told me, half unwillingly, I admit, that I guess I haven't said anything about to you, Tom."

"Then she confided her secrets to you, eh?" half chuckled Tom; though he saw his chum was in anything but a humorous frame of mind. "I remember you told me she felt very bitter toward all Germans because she had lost her mother when the *Lusitania* went down."

"Yes. But this had to do with her guardian," Jack continued.

"Oh, I see! Mr. Potzfeldt, Jack? You haven't felt favorably disposed toward that gentleman at any time since first meeting him."

"Neither have you, Tom, to tell the truth!" declared the other quickly. "In fact, as I remember it, both of us were pretty much inclined to believe he was a paid spy of the German Government, working on some line of dark business over in America. Well, he had to clear out in a hurry, Bessie told me."

"Did the authorities get track of his scheming work, and was he in danger of being arrested for plotting against Uncle Sam's interests as a neutral?" Tom asked.

"It may have been that; but Bessie wasn't sure about it. In fact, she seemed inclined to believe her guardian had some secret, which was

MORE WORK IN PROSPECT

in danger of being exposed. An old friend of her mother's was interesting himself in the matter. Given time, he might have made it uncomfortable for Carl Potzfeldt; and so the gentleman cleared out between two days."

"Taking Bessie with him!"

"Yes. They made as if to go to Chicago, but instead hurried to New York. When he came aboard at the last call he kept to his cabin for a time, until we were well away from land. There has been considerable of mystery about his actions. Bessie is afraid of him, too. She even hinted that she believed he might have obtained control of her fortune and herself through fraud, and that this was in danger of being found out at the time he cut stick and ran."

"All this is interesting, Jack; but just when and how we're ever going to learn the truth about it I'm unable even to guess. It would be like hunting for a needle in a haystack to try to find Potzfeldt. He and his pretty little ward may be hundreds of miles away from here."

"Perhaps you're right, Tom," mused the other sadly, as he stared afar off toward the north. "I'd be glad of a chance to do something for that poor girl. She is to be greatly pitied, if she's wholly in the power of a man who wouldn't hesitate to do *anything*, if he saw a chance for gain ahead."

"Well, all you can do, Jack, is to live on and hope a lucky chance will bob up for you. But there's our captain beckoning to me. Perhaps another battle is on the carpet for to-morrow, and I'll be given a look-in again."

"Oh, if the lightning would only strike me too!" sighed Jack, enviously. "Please beg him to figure out something I can do, Tom. If it's only occupying a place aboard an observation plane or taking photographs of the Germans regrouping far back of the lines, I'd gladly welcome it. Anything but sitting here, when all the other pilots are at work."

Tom hurried to join the commander of the Lafayette Escadrille. He had taken a great fancy to the gallant man, and believed this feeling was in a measure returned. Jack continued to sit and mope. He really felt slighted to be left out when so much thrilling work was being done.

He had put away the well-thumbed scrap of paper with its mysterious lines of warning, for the time being Bessie and all her troubles passing from his mind. Jack was now full of his own affairs. He found himself growing a bit discontented because thus far he had been allowed to do so little for the cause, when his

MORE WORK IN PROSPECT 107

heart was full to overflowing with a desire to assist.

There were aviators going and coming all the time, and surely many of them did not excel him appreciably in talents. Why did not those in charge find something for an ambitious pilot to do? He was striving daily to master the weak spots in his education; and had not the captain himself assured him he was doing bravely? He turned to cast an occasional look toward the spot where Tom and the commander of the air squadron still talked earnestly. Yes, something was certainly "on tap," as Jack expressed it, for he saw the other carefully examining a bit of paper his companion had evidently placed in his hand.

Jack began to be interested. Perhaps after all it might turn out to be something quite different from what Tom had anticipated. Had the captain simply wished to notify the other to be ready to answer a call on the following morning, surely he need not have taken all this time; nor would he have given Tom that paper, undoubtedly carrying explicit instructions.

How the minutes dragged! Jack thought it an eternity before he saw Tom and the captain separate. He was glad to notice that his chum once more headed in the direction of the spot where they had been seated on a bench back of the long row of frame buildings used for permanent hangars at the Bar-le-Duc aviation field.

Yes, Tom had evidently been told something that pleased him very much. His smile admitted the fact, and Jack knew by now just how to read the face of his comrade so as to get a good idea of what was passing in his mind.

"Looks like good news, Tom," he cried out, for motors were rattling and throbbing, mechanicians and helpers, as well as pilots, calling to one another, and all manner of sounds combining to make a great racket.

Tom shrugged his shoulders in a non-committal way, which might mean a whole lot, and again might express a small fraction of disappointment.

"Yes, I've been given a job, if that's what you mean," he admitted, as he dropped down once more on the bench alongside Jack, and threw one leg over the other.

"More fighting to-morrow, possibly?" queried Jack, anxiously. But he found his curiosity further whetted when Tom shook his head in the negative.

"Not necessarily this time, it seems," he went on to say; "though of course you never can tell what you'll strike when once you pass fifty miles, more or less, behind the enemy front."

Jack pursed his lips up as if about to whistle, but he made no sound. It was only a visible indication of surprise on his part—surprise, and an eager desire to know just what his chum was so slow in telling him.

"Another bombing raid, then, is it?"

"Never a bomb going along this time," came the puzzling answer. "Nor is there going to be a big bunch of planes starting out. I'm to be the only pilot in the game this time, Jack."

"You're knocking me silly with that, Tom," protested the other young aviator. "I can see the twinkle in your eyes, as if you were holding something back, so as to tantalize me. Are you free to tell me what this business of yours it is the captain has just handed over to you?"

"Oh, surely, Jack. He told me I could take *one* fellow into my confidence, and no more. So I mean to tell you all about it."

Tom turned and cast a careful look around. They were not very close to any of the hangars, it happened; and none of the many helpers and attendants could possibly overhear what was said, with all that clatter constantly going on.

"I guess it's perfectly safe for me to talk here, Jack, and not give the thing away. You know it does seem that the German spies are able to penetrate nearly everywhere, and pick up all sorts of valuable information, to send across the line in any one of a dozen different ways."

"Yes. But go on, Tom."

"It seems there is need of some one to go to-night to a particular place far back of the German lines—in fact, close to the fortified city of Metz itself. In a certain place, inside a hollow post, will be found a paper marked in cipher, and containing much valuable information which has been collected by one of the ablest of the French spies. He is really a native of Alsace-Lorraine, and well thought of by the Germans. As it is utterly out of the question for him to report in person, he has adopted this way of getting his news to General Petain. And as there is a scarcity of pilots capable of doing this work our captain has selected me to undertake it for the cause."

"But Tom, I should have thought he would have picked out some one more familiar with the ground back there. How can you find your way to that particular place, if you've never been there before?"

"I've been given directions that are bound to take me right," Tom assured his worried chum. "There was a man they used for this purpose, and several times he's brought back the papers; but on his last trip he had the misfortune to run into a bunch of cruising Fokkers, and they brought him down. He fell fortunately inside the French lines, so his papers were saved; but Francois will never handle the controls of a plane again. He was killed."

"Then there *is* danger in the game!"

"Certainly there is. But in these times who could dream of passing so far back of the German front without expecting to be in constant peril? The papers will be put in a little box previously prepared. Should disaster overtake us, it will be flung overboard, and before it reaches the ground everything will have been consumed by the fire that follows."

Jack's eyes began to glitter.

"Just so, Tom! But I notice that you used the plural pronoun when you spoke. Then you do not go on this mission alone?"

"No, that's right. I have been given permission to pick out my one companion, for there will be two of us aboard the plane to-night."

Jack tried to keep calm, but it was indeed difficult, and his voice faltered more or less as he hurriedly went on to say:

"Have you already made your selection?"

"Yes," the other assured him in his tantalizing way. "I wanted to know whether the captain approved of my choice; which I am glad to say turned out to be the case."

Jack gulped something down, and then blurted out:

"Did you mention my name at all, Tom?"

"Yours was the only one I had in mind; and Jack, rest easy, you're going along with me to-night to glimpse the lights of Metz!"

CHAPTER XIV

OFF ON A DARING MISSION

THE two air service boys fell to talking earnestly concerning what they should take with them, and how to study a map which their captain had promised to put in Tom's hands immediately.

This was not of the ordinary kind, but so definitely marked for just such an emergency that even a novice could probably find his way to Metz, granting that he possessed the necessary qualifications of an air pilot.

Presently a messenger came with a package for Tom. This proved to be the chart from the commander of the air squadron. Tom was to make as good a copy as was in his power, for the original was too valuable to risk losing.

Jack understood that there were several reasons for having Tom do this. In the first place his work on the chart would familiarize the young aviator with its every detail, and fix things firmly in his mind. Then again, if they were lost, and never returned, the priceless chart for night voyaging over the enemy's lines would be at least safe.

Daring men had gone forth on similar desperate errands before then, and had never been heard from again. It is the fortune of war. Those who indulge in enterprises that border on the sensational must always expect to sup with deadly peril.

When the evening meal was announced the two chums were already deep in the work. Of course not a whisper of their intended mission was breathed at the table. No one dreamed of their contemplated trip. The customary chatter and good-natured badinage flowed during the whole supper-time. While some of the American aviators had received wounds in recent engagements there had been no chair vacant for some little time now; and hence no gloom rested on the escadrille. From the table the boys again went to their room.

"How far is Metz from Verdun?" asked Jack, as they labored to complete their preparations for departure.

"Not over forty miles, I should say, as the crow flies, Jack. I've never been over the route, but it can be measured on this copy of the map."

"And that's the direct line we expect to cover, of course?"

"We'll head due east."

"And as it'll be densely dark when we start I guess we needn't mount to ten thousand feet to pass over the enemy lines, eh, Tom?"

"There'll really be little need," came the reply, showing that the pilot had already figured all this out. "At the same time we ought to keep far enough out of range to avoid being struck by stray shrapnel."

"Will they bombard us, do you think?" demanded Jack.

"Oh, that's to be expected," said Tom indifferently. "You see the men who man the anti-aircraft guns are constantly on the alert. They're bound to hear the whirr of our propeller as we pass over, no matter how high we soar. The searchlight will spot us out, and then they'll do their best to make things uncomfortable for the pair of us. But the chances are ten thousand to one against our being hit."

"You said our course would be due east, didn't you?"

"I'll change that assertion a bit, Jack; we start east after we're well across the front, and away from the dazzling searchlight business. In the beginning we'll point the nose of our big machine toward the north."

"So as to deceive the watchers, of course," remarked Jack.

"That's what the game is."

Jack's eyes sparkled. He was always proud of his chum's clever reasoning powers, and believed Tom could hold his own with any one with regard to mapping out a promising plan.

Their preparations completed, the two air service boys lay down to secure a little rest. As they were not to start until some time after midnight, Tom believed they should secure a few hours of sleep. The moon was a late one, and would not rise, even with a midnight start, until they were well back of the enemy lines.

An alarm-clock aroused them at the appointed time. Tom immediately shoved the noisy thing under his blankets before it could wake up the entire house, and set people wondering what was happening that any one should want to be aroused at such an unseemly hour.

It was terribly black outside. Jack pressed his nose against the window and took a look, even while hurriedly finishing his dressing. Tom had taken the precaution to put a fresh battery in his little hand electric torch, which he believed would prove to be worth its weight in gold.

Arriving at their destination, the boys quickly found their two-seater aircraft awaiting their coming. Quite a crowd stood around, and made guesses concerning the possible reason for the captain's order that this plane should be made ready for a journey, with enough supplies of gasolene and oil aboard to cover any ordinary emergency.

Tom took no chances. He believed the attendants had faithfully carried out all directions, but to make doubly sure he looked over things himself. It was his life and Jack's that were at stake, and not those of the attendants; so he persisted in testing this and that thing until he felt certain everything was as it should be.

"Is it time we started, Tom?" asked his companion, when this procedure had resulted satisfactorily.

"We'll wait just ten minutes more," he was told. "I've figured everything down to a fraction, and expect to proceed by clock-work. We want to be well over the line before the moon peeps up. After that we can loaf a bit, and let the old lady get a little way above the horizon. That's so we may have the benefit of her light when we want to land."

The minutes passed slowly. Meanwhile the crowd increased, every man who chanced to be abroad at that hour of the night gathering to see the two Americans start on their mysterious errand. All sorts of guesses were indulged in, many of them of the wildest character. Jack hearing some of this talk, which he half understood, was convulsed in silent laughter over the remarkable ideas that seemed to possess the minds of those French mechanicians and hostlers.

Finally Tom stood up.

"It's time!" he said simply, and Jack understood without any further explanation. He at once proceeded to climb into his seat and complete his simple preparations for the work in hand, being already fully dressed in his fur-lined garments, and with his warm hood and goggles in place.

A minute afterwards Tom called out the word that started the propellers whirling. The motor took up the refrain, and hummed merrily, as though glad to be busy again. Then they were pushed along for a start, gathering momentum so quickly that the mechanicians dropped back to watch the dark object vanish almost wholly from their sight along the level field.

Both boys noticed the great difference between this two-seater and their own active little Nieuports. How clumsy this machine was, and how slow to answer to the call of the pilot! Yet it would be far better for their purpose than two of the small aircraft, since it allowed them to be together.

The few lights of the aviation field near Bar-le-Duc had faded almost entirely out of sight by the time Tom turned to the north and headed for Verdun. True, he might have pointed the nose of the airplane directly east, and saved considerable distance, but there were good reasons for not doing this.

To cross the German lines further south would surely convince the Teutons that the aviators were heading for the vicinity of Metz, which was just what Tom did not wish to have happen. Then again, his chart covered only the direct line between Verdun and the fortified city of Lorraine that forty-odd years back had been French territory, before the Germans seized it as spoils after the war that made France a republic for the third time.

CHAPTER XV

THE MOONLIGHT FLIGHT

THE time for talking had passed. With the motor working noisily, and the twin propellers churning the air, they could hardly have heard the discharge of one of the Big Berthas', as the Allies were wont to call the monster Krupp guns, and so called them because a woman whose maiden name had been Bertha Krupp, owned a big interest in the works where they were manufactured.

All was dark around and below them. Above the stars shone, and gave a small amount of cold, cheery light. Tom had made a study of the heavens, and was able to steer by means of the stars. The aviator is often as much dependent on compass and heavenly bodies to shape his course as the sailor hundreds of miles away from land.

Tom was in no especial hurry. He had carefully thought out his plans, and meant to pass over Verdun at just a certain time. Then would come the two lines of hostile trenches, and the ordeal of searchlights and shrapnel. Once that was done with, they had really little further to fear.

The minutes slipped away. Under ordinary

THE MOONLIGHT FLIGHT 121

conditions they were accustomed to making that thirty miles in just about half that number of minutes, thanks to the ability of the speedy Nieuports to cover distance. It would be twice that now before they would find themselves at the front.

Already they could see various signs to tell them they were drawing near. Rockets used as signals of various kinds ascended at intervals, and burst. Others of the star variety, and which discharged glowing white electric balls that lighted the earth below, could also be seen. One side or the other apparently had some reason for desiring to scrutinize a special sector of terrain in No-Man's-Land, the disputed region lying between the hostile trenches.

Jack used his eyes to advantage. These things had not yet grown stale with him, for he still found himself filled with awe and wonder when gazing down from a lofty height at the world shrouded in darkness below.

There within a comparatively short distance, that might not be over twenty miles, a round million of soldiers were gathered, armed with numberless engines of destruction of the most ponderous nature imaginable. It was enough to give any one a genuine thrill, and Jack felt such a sensation creeping over him.

The crucial time had now come. They were

passing over the line of the French trenches. Jack knew this from various signs, and also that in another minute they might expect to be spotted by some of the enemy searchlights. These would be unmasked, and trained on the heavens in the effort to locate the cause of that well known clattering noise above.

This speedily came about. First one long shaft of dazzling light rushed back and forth; then others joined in the hunt, until presently they focussed on the progressing two-seater pushing north.

Then began the bombardment. Numerous anti-aircraft guns were poking their noses upward in anticipation of just such a call. Their crews commenced to shower the shrapnel around and below the bird of passage, whose mission, whatever it might prove to be, could mean only evil to the Teuton cause.

All this racket was lost upon the two so far above the earth. They heard nothing of the bleat of the firing guns. Even the bursting of shrapnel went unheeded, save at a time when a shell exploded close by, and was faintly heard.

Tom was wisely taking but little chance. He maintained an altitude that prevented most of the shrapnel from coming anywhere near the plane.

They crossed the enemy front, and sped on.

THE MOONLIGHT FLIGHT 123

The bombardment diminished in fury as they left the first and second line trenches behind them. It was continued to some extent from an elevation further back, but as Tom knew of this formation, and had crept up still higher, no accident happened to them.

At last the air service boys were fully launched on their night voyage through the upper currents. Tom waited until he considered that it was really safe to change their course. He did not want to betray his movements in case some daring Boche pilot started up in a swift Fokker machine to pursue them.

Once he shut off the engines and volplaned down a thousand feet or more. This was done because it was intensely cold up where they were; and the reasons that had kept them at such a high altitude existed no longer. Then again Tom wished to listen to discover if there was another aircraft near them; and this could be done only when his motor was silent.

"No pursuit, Jack!" he managed to call to his chum before they once more straightened out, and again allowed the motor to send forth its loud hum.

Jack had no chance to make any sort of reply. It did not matter, for he, too, had eagerly listened, and had failed to catch any telltale sound.

Immediately Tom shaped a new course. No longer were they heading toward the north by east, but directly east. There some forty miles, more or less, away, lay the city of Metz, the object of their mission.

After moving along in this fashion for a short time Tom drove his machine more slowly. He was watching for the rising of the old moon ahead, where the horizon was already lighted with her near approach.

How strange she looked peering above the edge of the world as though curious to see all that was going on in this troubled hemisphere. Jack thought he had never witnessed a more peculiar spectacle. But at least this fragment of a moon would be likely to afford them the necessary illumination required when they attempted to land in a field that neither of them had ever seen before, and only knew through information imparted by means of their chart, and its accompanying notes.

Some other pilot had doubtless been over this same route on previous occasions; yes, and even landed in that identical field. He had made the chart; and the accompanying memoranda consisted of his personal experiences.

Already the moon had dispelled some of the cheerless gloom round about them. It was still cold up in that upper strata of rarefied air;

but their fur-lined garments kept them from suffering. Besides this, they were young and vigorous, and their blood was warm, and they were excited with their mission and able to ignore any physical discomfort that might come to them.

Jack continued to stare ahead as time passed. He was looking for some sign of the city towards which they were flying. Tom, on his part, often took note of his compass, then flashed a glance up at the stars, and finally sought to discover some landmark far down below that was marked upon the chart.

He had the utmost confidence in his own judgment, and believed he would bring up at the identical place which was their goal.

Tom now volplaned again, wishing to draw nearer to the earth. It was while thus dropping, with engine muffled, that his ears caught a sound calculated to give him an uneasy feeling.

This was undoubtedly the whirr of a propeller beating the air in furious fashion. It also came from behind. Jack, too, had caught the sound, and was thrilled with sudden apprehension of impending trouble.

They were undoubtedly being pursued, and by a much faster plane than their own. This would mean that presently they would be overtaken and fired upon. It was not in the nature of Tom Raymond to allow such a thing to occur and be kept from doing his share of the fighting.

When Tom swung around to face the rear, and actually started to run toward the oncoming foe, Jack knew what was expected of him. He must man the gun, and prove how well he had learned his lesson when at school at Pau and at Casso.

No longer could they expect to be guided by sounds. Their own motor thundered so loudly that every other sound was deadened. They must depend on eyesight alone to tell them when they were nearing the oncoming Fokker craft. Perhaps the first indication they would have of its presence would be the flash of its quick-firing gun, spattering bullets around them like hail.

So Jack strained his vision to the limit. He was eager to discover the enemy before they themselves were seen. Much might depend on who fired first, in a duel of this kind.

Suddenly the gun began to bark after its own peculiar way. Jack believed he had glimpsed something moving, and was sending forth a storm of lead in the hope of a lucky hit that would crumple the other machine up and put an end to that peril.

Tom held the course. He knew that every

THE MOONLIGHT FLIGHT 127

second was carrying the rival airplanes nearer together — knew that possibly they were so headed that if they continued to rush forward they might smash in a frightful collision that would send both down thousands of feet to the earth.

It was a time for careful calculations and prompt action. Tom gripped the controls and was ready either to swerve or to dip as occasion demanded. Meanwhile, Jack was doing his best to riddle the advancing Boche machine and its pilot.

There was no longer any difficulty in seeing just where the Fokker was, for a constant flashing as her gun rattled betrayed its position exactly. The flying lead was now whistling all about the two air service boys but they did not know how close they sailed to death.

Then Tom swung smartly to the right. He dared not keep on longer in his course lest he collide with the German craft. Just about the same instant he realized that the Fokker was diving. There was something queer about that manoeuvre. Tom had never known a French or an American nor yet a British airman to adopt such a clumsy way of plunging so as to avoid punishment.

Circling around he started back on a little lower level, looking for the enemy. In making his latest volplane Tom had listened intently, hoping to ascertain whether the motor of the enemy craft still throbbed somewhere close by; but he heard not a sound to tell the story.

Just then, suspicious of the truth, he glanced down, and was just in time to see a little flash of flame arise from the distant surface of the earth. Then the awful truth broke upon both boys. They realized that the German pilot had lost control of his machine, which had turned over and over in its drop, finally crashing to the ground, and being instantly enveloped in flames!

CHAPTER XVI

LANDING CLOSE TO METZ

Tom had his hands full in trying to get back to his course again. Naturally, in the excitement attending the duel in midair he could not pay attention to where he was going. It was easy enough to shape his line of flight by the aid of the stars and his compass, but he had also to catch certain landmarks below, that would serve to guide him.

Fortune favored him in that he quickly sighted the lights of a town; and this gave him the bearings he sought. His mind freed from further anxiety concerning this matter, he pushed on once more.

When presently he became aware of the presence of more lights Jack gave Tom the signal agreed on between them to mark such a circumstance. Then the pilot again commenced to drop to lower levels by a series of easy volplanes.

Like a huge bird the airplane swept along, now close to earth. Had one of the peasants who lived in that region chanced to be aroused by the rattle of the propeller and thrust his head out of his cottage door, he must have gazed in awe to see the vast shadowy form come between him and the starry heavens, with the light of the moon silvering its extended wings.

One trip failed to show them just what they wanted, and so Tom, knowing that the field must be somewhere in that immediate neighborhood, immediately swung around and started in again.

The second search failed to bring success. Jack began to experience a sensation akin to dismay. Was their work doomed to meet with no result and would they find themselves compelled to start back to Verdun without having accomplished the important errand on which they had been dispatched?

It was not Tom Raymond's way to feel discouraged because things did not always go as he wished from the start. He believed in the old motto, "If at first you don't succeed, try, try again." And he would circle around that vicinity for a full hour if only in the end he might find that for which he searched.

Three times however, was the limit. Then Tom felt certain he had "struck pay dirt"; and that the opening lying below was the identical field to which he had been directed.

After that it resolved itself into a simple landing by moonlight. There were no ready mechanicians waiting to lend a hand; and everything must be done by the pilot and his assistant. But then, all war aviators must be able to make ordinary repairs if necessary, and do other duties that usually they allow the mechanics to perform.

Tom brought the heavy machine to the earth softly. It was fine work he did, considering the fact that it was unfamiliar ground he was striking and the moonlight was far from strong.

They jolted along a short distance, and then came to a full stop. Jack was the first to spring out. His first thought was of the strangeness of being on German soil, far back of the fighting lines, and within a few miles of Metz, a city of prime importance.

Hardly had they landed when the air service boys found themselves listening to sounds that seemed significant. Plainly came reports of firearms and of loud shouting, as of excited men.

"What do you think that row means, Tom?" asked Jack, as they stood listening with quickened hearts.

"It's hard to say," the other replied. "They may be having a riot of some kind over in the city. But I'm afraid it is more apt to have something to do with our presence here."

"Do you mean they've seen our dropping down and that there may be soldiers on the way here to see what we're up to?" asked Jack.

"That may turn out to be the truth of it. But we mustn't lose any more time. What we want now is that paper. Jack, remember that we arranged it so you'd stay with the plane, while I hurried off to get it."

"All right, Tom; only I wish you'd let me go along. Then if anything happened we'd be together, anyhow."

"It's better for you to stay here. I'll be gone only a few minutes if everything turns out O. K."

Tom turned and ran across the field. Jack stared after him until he lost track of the runner in the misty moonlight. Then he occupied himself in listening to that clamor and wondering whether it was really getting closer, or if his fears only made him think so.

There was certainly a big noise. Men continued to shout, and guns were being discharged, but not so frequently as before. Perhaps this latter was done by nervous guardians of the Lorraine city, who on first hearing the racket took it for granted that it meant an airplane attack, and were therefore starting in to bombard the skies, discovering hostile fliers in every lurking fleecy cloud.

Yes, Jack was positive now that those who

shouted to one another must be coming out of the city, and heading for the big field where Tom had dropped down.

"Like as not," Jack told himself, "some wisebody has discovered that airplanes have been using this ground for alighting. When they had word that an enemy machine was heading this way they just naturally concluded it might drop down here. I guess our little fight up aloft was heard and understood by some one on guard. I hope Tom will soon get back here, that's what!"

Tom had been gone several minutes, and Jack tried to pierce the misty light beyond in the endeavor to discover some sign of his returning. His uneasiness increased, and with reason, for the noise was drawing perilously near.

Jack tried to figure out what his plan of campaign should be in case a motley mob of citizens and soldiers suddenly appeared in view, carrying lanterns, and perhaps blazing torches.

True, he had his automatic pistol with him, but what would that puny weapon avail when pitted against a score or two of enemies; many of them armed soldiers of the Kaiser, who would ruthlessly fill him with lead at the first show of resistance on his part?

Would it be better policy for him to slip away and conceal himself in case they did arrive before Tom returned?

But had not Tom explicitly told him to stay on guard over the airplane until he came back? Jack drew in a fresh breath. He threw back his shoulders aggressively and his mind was made up. He would stick it out, no matter at what cost. If the Boches wanted that plane they would have to fight for it, that was all.

He had his pistol out now, and was fondling it as a child would a pet toy. So far Jack had fired the weapon only at targets, but he had the reputation of being a good shot. He believed he could make every bullet it contained tell.

Then what about the mitrailleuse aboard the plane? Was it not possible to train it on the advancing host, and give them such a hot reception that they would break and race madly for shelter?

He knew the gun was fixed to shoot straight ahead. This was the custom with all those who went up in airplanes. To attempt to fire any other way would imperil the stability of the plane, and in many cases bring about sudden disaster.

Jack fumbled for the fastenings of the airplane mitrailleuse, it being his intention to swing the gun free, so that he could turn its muzzle in any quarter desired. But it had been too well secured in place for such a quick delivery, and presently he gave the idea up as a bad one.

No Tom yet! Things certainly were taking on a dark hue, and it looked as though desperate trouble might be in store for the two chums. Jack almost believed he could see dancing lights coming along what might be a road. He looked again, and no longer had any doubt on that score.

"Well, a fellow can die only once, and after all what does it matter whether he meets his end by falling ten thousand feet from the clouds or in trying to hold off an angry mob of Teuton soldiers and citizens of Metz who are in sympathy with the methods of the Kaiser?" Jack's reflections served to give him courage.

There was the leading one of the mob, starting across the dimly lighted field! Jack set his jaws hard, and determined that he would wait until the other had come close up. Ammunition was much too precious to be wasted without results following.

He was soon glad he had made such a sensible resolution, for as the runner drew closer something familiar about his figure and methods of leaping told Jack it was none other than Tom.

"Get aboard in a hurry, after you've given the propellers a swing!" cried Tom, almost breathless himself after such a sharp run. "I've got what I wanted."

He was already in his place with his hand on the control.

"Tell me when, Tom!" sang out Jack.

"Cut loose!" ordered the pilot.

The propellers spun, and the motors commenced their furious throbbing. Jack swung aboard, and at once the plane started to roll along the field, even as men appeared, bursting into view on one side, and shouting harshly as they realized how close they had come to catching those they sought.

CHAPTER XVII

MORE TROUBLE FOR THE CHUMS

It had been a close call for the two air service boys. Had they been delayed just a minute or two longer escape might have been impossible. And to have been caught with the spy's paper of information in their possession might have proved a very serious matter.

Some of the mob, that had come from Metz itself, were German soldiers. They carried guns with which they opened a hot fire on the departing plane.

Again the lucky star of Tom and Jack seemed to be in the ascendant, for they did not receive even a scratch. Later they found reason to believe that a number of the leaden missiles had come very close to their persons; for the marks upon the body of the plane itself, as well as the tiny holes in the stout linen covering of the wings, told where bullets had passed. Possibly, though, these had come from the rapid-fire gun handled by the Boche airman.

The plane had left the ground and started to mount when this shooting occurred, so that the marksmen had at least had a fair target at which to fire. But as the departing airplane was speeding away from them the rapidly increasing distance may have disconcerted the Germans. At any rate they failed to bag their game.

The boys were now mounting upwards again, filled with joy over their recent escape. Jack felt sure that Tom had the precious paper; for he well knew the other would never have returned so quickly had not success rewarded his search.

They were soon heading directly for their distant base. Tom could not give his aerial steed the rein, and get all the speed possible out of the cumbersome two-seater. There was no longer any necessity for "loafing on the job," to allow a tardy moon to come in sight, as had been the case before. Home, and at top speed, was the slogan now.

But, alas! it was not long before Tom realized that something was wrong with the plane. He found it increasingly difficult to manage the engine, and the machine began to give erratic jumps that alarmed Jack.

Had it been possible to make himself heard above the clatter of the motor and the propeller, Jack would have been much inclined to shout out, and ask his more experienced comrade what had happened.

Still he could give a shrewd guess. One of the bullets fired by the Teuton soldiers must have struck some part of the motor, and done enough damage to make its workings exceedingly erratic. If such were the case, would it be wise for them to try to push on at this high altitude, where a sudden collapse would mean death for both of the occupants of the disabled plane?

Tom soon shut the motor off, and tilted the machine for a volplane down several thousand feet to a new level.

Jack held his breath. This was partly because the wind rushed at him in a vicious fashion while they were plunging downward, and also on account of a new fear that clutched his heart.

How about the wings of the airplane standing the strain when Tom suddenly brought that volplane to a stop and tried to sail on an even keel again? Would they hold out? Or had some defect occurred in them which could also be charged to the spattering bullets fired by the Metz mob?

Then Jack breathed easier again.

The thing had been accomplished, and they were once more speeding onward, as Tom touched the controls that started the motor working. All then was well, as far as they had gone. Apparently they could by successive stages descend close to the treetops, and skim along until some favorable open space showed, into which a skillful pilot would find it possible to drop lightly and land.

A second volplane further added to Jack's peace of mind. They were now half-way down, and all seemed well. The earth loomed up below, although as yet it took on only a vague, misty effect, due to the weak moonlight.

Jack busied himself in trying to make things out, as for the third time the nose of the heavy observation Caudron was suddenly pointed downward, and they took the next "header."

This time Tom dropped a greater distance. When once more the loud hum of motor and propellers was heard they had almost reached the treetops. Jack gave one gulp, in fear lest his pilot could not make things work as he intended, and that they must crash to the earth while descending at such frightful speed.

Now everything was all right. They could not be more than a thousand feet above the floor of the valley they were following in their homeward route. If anything happened surely Tom would find some way of making a landing, even if a clumsy one that would put their machine out of the running and leave them stranded on enemy soil.

They continued to move along slowly, both looking eagerly to discover signs that would invite a possible landing. It looked as though they were in the country; at least they did not discover any signs of lights to indicate the presence of houses near by.

Soon a landing proved feasible, as they came to just the kind of open plot the air service boys yearned to discover. To make absolutely certain before committing himself, Tom circled the ground twice, and even dropped lower and lower while so doing, all the while straining his vision to the utmost.

Then the thing was done.

That was far from a pleasant landing. It shook them up considerably; but Jack was of the opinion that no damage resulted to the airplane, which after all was just then the main consideration.

Both of them leaped to the ground, after which Tom secured his electric hand-torch which he had found useful so many times while on the outward trip and he wished to consult the compass or the register of the barograph.

"I guess there's some sort of a house near by," said Jack, "because a rooster crowed over yonder. Yes, I can see what looks like the line of a road, too. I suppose it runs the entire length of this valley.

While Jack was saying this softly the pilot had started to take an inventory of the motor.

His now practiced eye ran along this and that part, each of which was so essential to the smooth running of the engine. Tom too had already formed a pretty clear idea as to where he was likely to find the damage, and hence was able in a short time to give a satisfied grunt.

"Located the trouble, have you, Tom?" queried the other.

"Yes. It's right where I expected to find it. A bullet has made a dent that interferes with the free action of the part. Besides, I think that spark plug has become fouled with oil, and will have to be changed to get the best results."

"How lucky you brought another with you! Lots of fellows wouldn't have bothered about such a little thing."

"I had my suspicions about that when we started," explained the other, "even though the mechanician assured me it was perfectly clean. I know different now, and will certainly give him a piece of my mind when we get back."

"Then you expect to get home safely, do you?" asked Jack, in a relieved tone, that proved how anxious he had been growing since troubles had so consecutively alighted on them.

"Surely," chuckled the other, with his usual confidence in voice and manner, "a thing like this isn't going to stop our plans. Here in this retired spot nobody's apt to bother us while we make our repairs. You can hold this torch, Jack, and shove the light squarely on the work."

Tom worked for some time. He tapped as gently as possible when knocking out the dent made by the bullet, and he gradually removed the cause of the trouble. He was just finishing with the spark-plug when the confidence of the air service boys received a sudden jolt.

CHAPTER XVIII

THE LONE HOUSE BY THE ROADSIDE

"LISTEN, Tom!" hissed Jack.

The other had just sighed with relief on completing the work of replacing the sparkplug that had become fouled with oil.

"I, too, heard it plainly, Jack!" he breathed.

"Was it someone screaming or sobbing?" asked the other breathlessly.

"Sounded like it to me."

"And either a woman or a girl, at that!" hazarded his chum in bewildment.

"It might have been a boy," suggested Tom. "There it is again."

Both of them listened. Peculiar sensations crept over them as they stood and thus strained their ears to catch any further sounds. Sobbing at any time is enough to arouse the feelings of a sensitive nature; but heard in the dead of night, and under the conditions that surrounded the two young aviators, made it all the more thrilling.

Jack in particular was touched to the heart.

"Say, that's a queer thing, Tom!" he muttered. "Why should anybody be crying or screaming like that away off here, and at this time of night?"

LONE HOUSE BY THE ROADSIDE 145

"Oh, there are many who are weeping in these dark days," said Tom gravely. "The men in myriads of families will never come home again. Perhaps a mother, or it may be a sister, has just had word that son, father, or brother has been shot down in battle."

Jack shuddered. Why should his thoughts instantly fly to the Boche pilot whom they had met and fought and conquered while on the way to Metz on their present perilous mission? It had been a fair fight, and a case of their lives or his. Nevertheless Jack shuddered as he remembered how the other had gone down after that last exchange of gunfire.

"Tom, notice that it comes from almost the identical direction where I told you I heard the crowing of a rooster a while ago," he hastened to say, more to rid his mind of those ghastly thoughts than anything else.

What a strange fatality if this should be the home of the unfortunate Teuton pilot of that Fokker machine, and the one who mourned was his mother or a young sister, or perhaps his wife!

"That means there's a house not far away, possibly an estate of some kind," mused Tom, as though turning over some sudden project in his mind.

Jack guessed what his chum was thinking about.

"Tom," he said softly, when for the third time they caught the heart-rending, half stifled sobs coming on the still night air.

"What do you want now, Jack?"

"I was just wondering whether you'd agree to something," continued the other, in a persuasive tone. "We're not in any *great* hurry, are we?"

"Well, no, perhaps not, Jack; though I'd like to deliver the paper into the hands of our commander as soon as possible. It is probably of the utmost importance, you know."

"I can't help thinking how I'd feel, Tom, if my mother or sister were in some great trouble, and fellows who might be in a position to hold out a helping hand considered their own personal safety first."

When Jack said this his voice was husky. Apparently the incident appealed strongly to his emotions. Jack had always been unusually thoughtful in regard to women of whatever age or degree, and would go far out of his way to do one a favor; so it was not strange that he should feel as he did at this time.

Tom was in a mood to be easily persuaded. The plaintive sobs, telling of woe that clutched some one's heart-strings, stirred a responsive chord within him. He, too, remembered those at home. Jack had put a clincher on his argu-

LONE HOUSE BY THE ROADSIDE 147

ment when he asked what their opinion of a man would be who turned aside and went his own way after hearing a woman or a child crying bitterly.

"All right, then, Jack; perhaps we can spare the time to take a turn around here, and see if we can be of any help," he announced, greatly to the satisfaction of his chum.

"Perhaps some one has been hurt and needs assistance," suggested Jack. "It isn't going to delay us much, and may be of great help to them. Come on—let's be on the move."

Tom was not quite so precipitate as his companion. Caution had a part in his make-up.

"Don't try to rush things, Jack," he said. "I must take a last look over my work here, you know."

"But you said everything was completed, Tom!" persisted the other.

"So it is, but I ought to make doubly sure before we leave the plane," Tom added, as he took the electric hand-torch from his companion and began systematically to look over the engine at which he had been working, carefully examining every detail.

Jack said nothing further. He understood what his chum meant when he declared it important that they should know absolutely the motor was in prime condition for immediate service. Something might occur to necessitate a hurried departure from the vicinity; a detachment of the enemy forces might appear, or other perils hover over their heads that might be laughed at only if they could take to the air without detention.

Tom was not long in doing as he desired. Meanwhile Jack could hear an occasional sob from the same quarter as before, and the sounds continued to exercise a peculiar influence over him which he could not have explained had he been asked.

"I'm ready now, Jack!"

"Glad to hear it," muttered the other, half under his breath; not that he meant to infer Tom had been unduly long, but because his feelings were wrought up to a high pitch that caused him to quiver all over.

Tom evidently guessed this, judging from his next remark.

"Cool down, Jack," he said, laying a hand on his companion's arm. "This will never do, you know. Getting excited is the worst thing an air pilot can do. It'll prove fatal to all your hopes, unless you manage to control your feelings better."

"I guess you're right, Tom."

"I don't think there's any chance the plane will be discovered here in the open field, even if

LONE HOUSE BY THE ROADSIDE 149

there is a road so close by," mused the pilot, after they had gone perhaps as far as twenty-five yards.

"Not in a thousand years," asserted Jack confidently, turning to look back as he spoke. "Why, even now I can't discover a sign of the wings, or anything else in the misty moonlight, it's so deceptive. Only that lone tree standing close to where we dropped tells me the location of our plane."

"Yes, I marked that, too," asserted Tom quietly. "I thought we ought to have some sort of landmark to guide us if we should be in a hurry coming back. And the tree, standing up fairly high, can be seen ten times better than anything close to the earth."

"Here's the road, Tom."

"So it is, and an important one in the bargain, judging from its condition," remarked the other, softly.

"It runs the length of the valley, of course," added Jack. "I shouldn't be surprised if it went all the way from Metz to the Verdun front. If that's the case it must have considerable travel, even if nothing has chanced to come along since we landed."

"I can see signs to tell that we are close to some sort of country estate, or it may only be a Lorraine farm."

"I can glimpse lights through the trees, and chances are they come from windows in the house beyond."

"I see them too," affirmed Tom.

"But say, isn't it pretty late for a farmhouse to be lighted up like that?"

"Depend on it, there's some good reason for all that illumination," Jack was told. "And perhaps we'd better drop this talking so much, now we're getting close to the place. No telling what we'll find there. For all we know this may be some one's headquarters, though pretty far back of the line for that sort of thing. But I think it'll turn out to be something more than ordinary."

It did.

Jack began to weave all manner of fantastic explanations to account for the illumination of the house alongside the road to Metz.

He felt he would not be very much astonished to discover a line of military cars standing at the gate, and find that an important council of war was being conducted within the building.

Then he remembered the crying and sobbing. Somehow, that did not seem to fit in with his other imaginings. The touch of Tom's hand on his arm made Jack give a violent start.

"Here's a high fence, you notice," Tom whispered. "Seeing that makes me believe it's going to turn out to be a country estate, and not just a farm. We ought to find a gate somewhere further along."

"That crying has stopped, Tom."

"For the time being, yes," admitted the other. "Perhaps she's only gone away from the open window. I was in hopes it would keep on, so we could be guided straight."

Two minutes later, after walking alongside the high fence for some distance, they discovered the entrance to the place. Tom flashed his light on the ground.

"Been considerable going in and coming out of vehicles, generally automobiles," he announced.

"And private cars are almost taboo in all Germany these dark days, they tell us," mentioned Jack sagely. "That makes it look as if some sort of military business might be transacted in this isolated place. Gee! I tell you it's getting my curiosity whetted to a fine point, all this mystery. But we're going in, of course, Tom?"

"Some way or other, Jack. If the entrance is closed and locked we can climb over the fence, all right. But no need of worrying about that, because I already see the gates are ajar. Come on."

So they slipped into the enclosed grounds,

actuated by an impulse, wholly unconscious of what might be awaiting them. They had been drawn into the adventure simply on account of a praiseworthy desire to be of service to some unknown one who seemed to be in trouble. And neither of the boys even vaguely suspected as yet what strange happenings would confront them before many minutes passed by.

CHAPTER XIX

A NEST OF SPIES

NEITHER of the air service boys had any doubts now with regard to the character of the grounds they were invading at dead of night. It must be a private estate. Once it may have been kept up through a lavish expenditure of money, but of late years things had evidently been allowed to grow more or less wild.

Tom was following what appeared to be the drive. It was not difficult to do so, because of the moonlight that sifted down through the bare branches of the neighboring ornamental trees, now destitute of foliage.

The house was presently discovered. Just as Tom anticipated, it was a rather large building, that might even be called a mansion, or château. It lay half buried amidst a prodigious growth of trees and bushes.

Jack fancied there was a sort of haunted air about the place, something uncanny, as he told himself. And then those sobs or screams could not be forgotten.

"Let's go around first, and see what lies in the rear," whispered Tom.

He had an object in view when he said this. Having noted carefully their route in coming from the open field where they had left their big plane, Tom knew that the window from whence the sobbing had come must be either at the back of the house, or on the eastern side.

He was heading in that quarter now, and looking for signs of a light in some upper window. This he discovered speedily, and pointed it out to his companion.

"Whoever was crying, Jack, must be up there," he said, close to the other's ear so as to insure safety.

"But how can we find out?" queried Jack. "If you say the word I'm willing to climb up, and learn what's wrong."

"Not yet. We must take a turn around, and pick up more knowledge of this place, as well as the people who live in the house."

"Then why not creep up and look in at that lower window?" suggested Jack, pointing as he spoke. "I've seen a shadow passing back and forth, as if some person were walking up and down like a caged tiger. It's a man, too, Tom, because I could easily make out his figure, a tall man to boot."

Tom led the way, with Jack at his heels. They managed to crawl through the bushes that cluttered the ground close to the wall of the stone building, and were at length in a position to raise themselves from their knees and peep under the drawn shade.

Jack was the first to look. Almost instantly he drew back with a low ejaculation of wonder. Tom, spurred on by this fact, also raised his head until his eyes were on a level with the small strip of open space just below the shade. He too had a thrill at what he saw.

"I feel as if I must be dreaming!" whispered Jack huskily. "Tell me, is that man in there really Carl Potzfeldt, the good-for-nothing guardian of little Bessie Gleason?"

"It's no other than our old acquaintance of the Atlantic liner," admitted Tom, though he himself had some difficulty in believing the startling fact.

This man, whom they felt sure was a German spy, had last been seen descending the gangway from the steamer at an English port, with Bessie Gleason, his pretty little ward, held by the hand, as though he feared she might try to run away from him.

Many times had Jack tried to picture the conditions under which he might run across Carl Potzfeldt again; but no matter what line of flight his imagination took he certainly had never dreamed of such a thing as this. Here in the heart of Lorraine, many miles back of the German front, on a moonlight night, and in a lonely country house, he once more beheld the object of his former detestation.

He clutched his chum by the arm almost fiercely.

"Well, that settles it, Tom!" he muttered savagely.

"Settles what?" whispered the other, for the window was closed, and there did not seem to be any chance of their low-voiced exchange of opinions being overheard.

"I don't leave here until I've seen *her*. For if he's at this place it stands to reason Bessie must be here also. Tom, that was Bessie we heard sobbing, I just know it now."

Tom had already jumped to the same conclusion. Nevertheless he did not mean to let it interfere with his customary caution. Nothing was to be gained through reckless and hurried action. They must go slowly and carefully. This house by the roadside on the way to Metz he concluded might be a nest of spies, perhaps the headquarters of a vast network of plotters.

"Hark! There's a car coming along the road and stopping at the gates here!" he told his chum, as he drew Jack down beside him. "We must be more careful how we look in lighted windows. If any one chanced to be abroad in the grounds we'd be seen, and perhaps fired on."

They crept from the vicinity of the window. Tom led the way toward the front of the house, as if he had an object in view. The car was now coming in along the crooked drive. They could see its one light, for economy in the use of all means for illumination was a cardinal feature of the German military orders in those days of scarcity.

The car stopped in front of the house, and a man jumped out. Tom saw that he wore a uniform of some sort, and judged that he might be a captain, at least. There was a second figure on the front seat, also in the dark-green garb of a soldier, but a private possibly.

The two young Americans crouched amidst the dense bushes and listened. So many thrilling things were happening in rapid succession that their pulses beat with unwonted speed.

Before this the sound of the approaching car must have reached the ears of the man they had seen pacing the floor in the spacious room that looked like a library. There were many books in cases and on shelves, while pictures and boars' heads decorated the walls.

Potzfeldt opened the door just as the officer alighted, and there was an exchange of stiff military salutations. Tom discovered that his guess was a true one, for the man of the house addressed the other as "Captain."

It was too bad that they spoke in German as they stood by the open door. Jack for once bitterly regretted the fact that he had never taken up the study of that language when at school, as he might have done easily enough. It would have paid him handsomely just then, he believed.

The two men talked rapidly. Apparently the officer was asking questions, and demanding something, for in another minute Carl Potzfeldt took an object out of a bill book and handed it to the other. As near as the watchers could make out this object was a slip of paper, very small, but handled as though it might be exceedingly precious.

Jack had a sudden recollection of a correspondingly minute slip of paper which he and Tom had found hidden in that little receptacle attached to the leg of the homing pigeon the latter had shot.

More talk followed between the two men. Presently the man turned and hastened inside again. He had left the door standing open, however, with the German officer waiting as if for something he had come after besides the scrap of paper.

Jack knew now that the man in uniform was

A NEST OF SPIES

from the headquarters of the Crown Prince. That accounted for the numerous marks of cartires which Tom had discovered on the drive. This lonely house by the roadside on the way to Metz was a nest of spies. Perhaps Carl Potzfeldt might be the chief, through whom negotiations were conducted and lesser agents sent forth.

Jack had got no further in his deduction when he saw the tall man returning. He carried a bundle that was wrapped in a cloth, and depended from his hand by means of a heavy cord, or some sort of handle.

This he set down on the landing, while he passed further words with the captain; and now it was Potzfeldt who asked the questions, as though he wished to learn how things were going at the front.

Between queries and guttural replies the hidden air service boys heard a series of sounds that gave them sudden light. Jack's hand pressed on Tom's arm, as though in this manner he wished to call the attention of the other to the noise.

Many times both of them had listened to similar sounds while watching some pigeon on the barn roof dare a rival to combat, or when wooing his mate. And as they could easily trace this to the covered package which Carl

Potzfeldt had just brought out of the house, the meaning was obvious.

Of course there were pigeons in that cage, homing pigeons at that, like the one Tom had shot! Doubtless had that one escaped its tragic fate the message it carried would have been delivered to the owner of this lonely house, in turn to be handed over to one of the messengers from German headquarters.

And now the German captain, stooping over, took possession of the cage containing at least two of the trained birds. They would be carried to some point from which, on another night, a daring Boche airman would attempt to take them far back of the French front, to hand over to the agent who was in communication with the master spy, Carl Potzfeldt.

It was all very simple. Nevertheless it was also amazing to realize how by what might be called a freak of fate the air service boys had been enabled to discover these facts. But for the accident to the motor they would not have dreamed of making a landing short of the aviation field at Bar-le-Duc. Then, had they not caught that woeful sound of loud sobbing, the idea of looking around would never have occurred to them.

The officer was now starting back to his car, which would carry him post-haste to German headquarters, where the fresh message in a cipher code from beyond the French lines might be translated, and the valuable information it possibly contained be taken advantage of.

Presently the military chauffeur started to swing around a curve that would allow them to leave the grounds by the same gates through which they had entered. The car's course could be followed by the strong ray its one light threw ahead; and the boys were able to tell when it reached the road again.

As they expected it returned the same way it had come, probably heading for the headquarters of the Crown Prince.

CHAPTER XX

JACK CLIMBS A WALL

"What luck we're in to be here, Tom!" murmured Jack.

Carl Potzfeldt had again entered the house and closed the door; and the air service boys could no longer hear the car speeding along the road. Jack was quivering all over with excitement. The events that had just come to their attention filled him with a sensation of wonder approaching awe.

"It certainly is strange how we've stumbled on this nest of spies," admitted Tom.

"And the paper he gave the captain — it must have been a message in cipher that an incoming pigeon brought from back of our lines, eh, Tom?"

"I guess it was, Jack. We could see it was only a small scrap of paper, thin paper at that; but both of them handled it as if it were pretty valuable."

Jack was chuckling, such a queer proceeding that Tom could not help noticing it, and commenting on it.

"What's struck you as funny now?" he asked, puzzled to account for this sudden freak on the part of his companion.

"I was wondering," explained Jack, "whether that mightn't be the doctored message we believed our commander meant to send through some time or other with one of the pigeons we got that day we went hunting."

"That's possible," Tom agreed, also amused at the thought. "But then, whether it is or not, it means nothing to us, you understand. We are here, and must decide on our movements. If that was a bogus message, and will coax the Germans to make an attack at a certain place where a trap has been laid, that's their lookout."

"Somewhere about here must be the pigeon loft where those homing birds have been bred," suggested Jack, following up a train of thought.

"Yes, it may be on the flat roof of the château, or in the barn at the rear," Tom admitted. "One thing is certain, they know only this place as home; and wherever they're set free their first instinct is to strike a bee-line for here. Some people are so foolish as to fancy homers can be sent anywhere; but that's silly. It's only home that they're able to head straight toward, even if hundreds of miles away."

"Oh Tom! how about Bessie?" inquired Jack eagerly.

His chum considered, while he rubbed his chin with thumb and finger in a thoughtful way he had when a little puzzled.

"It might be done in a pinch," he finally muttered.

"What, Tom?"

"She's such a little mite that her weight wouldn't amount to much, if only she had the nerve to do it, Jack."

"Do you mean that you'd be willing to carry Bessie off with us? To help her escape from her guardian? I'm sure he must be treating her badly, or else she wouldn't be sobbing her poor little heart out, as we heard her."

"That would have to depend a whole lot on Bessie."

"As far as that goes I know she's a gritty little person," Jack instantly remarked. "Many times she said to me she wished she were a boy so that she might also learn to fly and fight for France against the detested Kaiser. Why, she even told me she had gone up with an aviator who exhibited down at a Florida resort, one having a hydro-airplane in which he took people up. And Bessie declared she didn't have the least fear."

"That sounds good to me, Jack."

"Then let's get busy, and try to let her know we're here," continued Jack.

"First of all, we'll get under the open window where she must have been standing at the time we heard her crying. I think I saw a movement up there while the two men were conversing on the porch. Perhaps Bessie was listening to what they said."

Tom's words gave his chum a new thought.

"Oh, it would certainly be just like Bessie to do it! She seemed to be full of clever ideas."

Tom, being mystified by such words, he naturally sought further information.

"What would she do?" he demanded.

"Send me that mysterious message by the little hot-air balloon," Jack announced with a vein of pride in his voice, feeling delighted over having solved the puzzle that had baffled him for so long.

"It hardly seems probable," Tom answered softly. "At the same time it isn't altogether impossible."

"How far are we from the French front, do you think, Tom?" pursued his comrade, determined to sift the whole thing out.

"Twenty miles or so, I should imagine."

"That isn't very far. Once I caught just such a little balloon in a tree in our yard that had a tag on it, telling that it had been set free in a village that lay *seventy* miles off. The wind had carried it along furiously, so that it covered all that distance before losing buoyancy, and coming down in the heavy night air."

"Yes, I know of other circumstances where such balloons have traveled long distances before falling. Then again, Jack, this valley extends pretty much all the way to the Verdun front, and the current of air would carry a balloon along directly toward our home patch."

"Oh, Bessie sent it, believe me!" asserted Jack again, more confidently than ever. "And she'll tell us so too, when she gets the chance."

Thus whispering the air service boys arrived at that side of the house where the lighted window on the second floor seemed to indicate that the object of their present concern could be found.

Tom examined the building as well as the limited amount of light allowed. He could easily see that any agile young fellow, himself or Jack for instance, might scale the wall, making use of some projections, and a cement flower trellis as well, in carrying out the project.

"We might throw pebbles up, and bring her to the window," he suggested, though pretty confident at the time Jack would find fault with such an arrangement.

"That wouldn't help her get down here to us, Tom," protested the other. "And that's what we're planning, you remember; for you said she could accompany us if she felt equal to it. I must go up myself and help Bessie get down. There's nothing else to do, Tom."

It looked very much as though Jack was right. Tom admitted this to himself; at the same time he wished there were some other way by means of which the same end could be gained, or that he could undertake the thing, instead of his comrade.

But to this Jack would never agree. Bessie was his own particular friend; and they had been most "chummy" while aboard the Atlantic liner crossing the submarine infested ocean. Then again that warning had been addressed to him, and not to both, showing that the writer had only been concerned about the danger he, Jack, was running, should his plane be tampered with by some emissary of Carl Potzfeldt.

"All right then; you go, Jack! But be careful about your footing. If you fell it'd be a bad thing in many ways, for even if you escaped a broken neck or a fractured leg you'd arouse the house, and all sorts of trouble would drop down on us in a hurry."

"Don't worry about me, Tom. I'll show you I'm as nimble as any monkey. Besides, that isn't much of a climb. Why, I could nearly do it with one arm tied fast."

"Go to it!" Tom told him, settling back to

watch the performance and give whispered advice if it seemed necessary.

Jack waited no longer. He was wild to find himself once more face to face with the pretty young girl in whom he had taken such an interest. Her recent sobs and cries still haunted his heart, and he felt certain she must be in great sorrow over something.

He commenced climbing. While his boast about being equal to any monkey that ever lived among the treetops may have been a bit of an exaggeration, all the same Jack was a very good athlete, and especially with regard to feats on the parallel bars or the ladders in a gymnasium.

He made his way nimbly upward, with Tom's eyes following every movement. It seemed an easy task for the climber. Just what he would discover when he had gained the open window was another question.

The light still remained, for which both boys felt glad. It afforded Jack a goal which he was striving to gain; and it told Tom further down that the inmate of the upper room was awake and still moving about, though her sobs had ceased.

Once Tom fancied he heard something stirring back of the house. He hoped it might not prove to be a servant attached to the

JACK CLIMBS A WALL 169

Potzfeldt place or an attendant who had charge of the pigeon loft.

Jack was almost up now. He had only to cover another yard of space when he could look into the room of the lighted window. That was where fresh peril must lie, because his figure would be outlined in silhouette, and any one moving about the grounds might discover that uninvited guests had arrived.

Tom wished he had told his chum to insist that the light be immediately extinguished, if, as they believed, it proved to be Bessie who occupied that room. He hoped his chum would think of it without being told.

There! At last Jack had arrived, and without accident! Now he was cautiously thrusting his head up a little, to peer within.

Tom held his breath. So much depended on what would follow Jack's betrayal of his presence.

"Tell her to put out the light, first of all, Jack!" Tom gently called out, using both hands as a megaphone to carry the sounds.

It seemed that he must have been heard, and his directions understood, for immediately there was another movement above, after which the illumination ceased, as though Bessie had blown out the lamp.

Tom breathed easier, though he still continued to look, and wonder how his chum was going to get the girl safely down from her elevated apartment. Jack was not so fertile in expedients as his chum, and many times depended on Tom to suggest ways and means.

While Tom was still waiting, and hoping for the best, he heard his comrade whisper down to him as he hung suspended, clutching the sill of the open window.

"After all, you'll have to come up too, Tom," he was saying feverishly. "There are complications that'll need your judgment, knots to untangle that are beyond me."

CHAPTER XXI

IN THE OLD LORRAINE CHÂTEAU

WHAT Jack said in his cautious fashion puzzled Tom. For the life of him he could not understand what had arisen, calling for any unusual display of generalship. Surely Jack should have been equal to the task of getting Bessie down from the window, even if he had to make use of knotted bed-clothes in lieu of a rope.

Still he had asked Tom to come up, and there was nothing to do but grant his request. "Complications," Jack said, had arisen. That was a suggestive word, and to Tom's mind seemed to hint at further mystery.

Accordingly he proceeded to imitate the example of his comrade. Jack had shown the way, and all his chum had to do was to follow. As Tom was also an all-around athlete, accustomed to much climbing from small boyhood, after nuts and birds' nests and all such things as take lads into tall trees, he found but little trouble in making the ascent.

When he drew himself alongside Jack, the other gave a sigh of relief.

"Whee! I'm glad you've come, I tell you, Tom," he said. "It was getting too big a job for me to tackle."

"What's happened, Jack?" asked the late arrival on the stone ledge under the window of the upper room.

"First, here's Bessie, Tom," Jack went on. "She wants to shake hands with you. Since we parted, when the steamer was docked, the poor girl has been having all sorts of trouble; and she's glad as can be to see us both again; aren't you, Bessie?"

Tom, feeling a small, trembling hand groping for his, immediately grasped it, and gave a squeeze that must have carried conviction to the heart of the girl.

"Oh, I'm shivering like everything!" she murmured, adding quickly: "But not with fear. It's because my prayers have been answered, and help has come at last, when everything looked so awfully dark—and I'm so very, very hungry."

"Hungry!" repeated Tom, starting, it seemed such a very strange word for the girl to use, even though they were in Germany, where all food he knew must be getting exceedingly scarce.

"Yes, what do you think, that rotten bounder of a spy is half starving the poor girl! He

IN THE OLD LORRAINE CHÂTEAU 173

ought to be tarred and feathered, that's what!" growled the indignant Jack.

"Not so loud," warned Tom. "Some one may hear you, Jack. But tell me what you've learned."

"Why, first of all, Tom, it was Bessie who wrote that warning message I had, and attached it to that little balloon, hoping the favorable breeze would carry it over the front to the French lines. So that mystery is explained. Then, Tom, there are *two* we've got to take out of this place, instead of just one, as we thought."

"I don't get you!" Tom ejaculated. "What do you mean by two?"

"It's a story in itself, I guess," whispered Jack. "I don't wholly understand it myself. But it seems that Bessie's mother didn't drown after all when the *Lusitania* went down, as Potzfeldt reported she did."

"You surprise me, Jack! How could that be?" demanded the other youth, thrilled by the startling information.

"Oh, that slick rascal managed it somehow," came the soft if indignant reply. "We'll learn more about it later on. He was picked up by a fishing boat. The lady was temporarily out of her mind, so he gave it out later that she had gone down. How he ever got her over here in Germany beats me. But he managed to do it it seems. And she's been kept a prisoner in this old château of his ever since!"

"But what was his object?" asked the amazed Tom.

"It had a heap to do with finances," Jack told him. "While he held a paper that gave him charge over her daughter over in America, and a part of the big Gleason fortune also, there were valuable papers he had been unable to get his greedy hands on. She absolutely refused to tell him where they were hidden. As a last resort what did the wretch do but go all the way back to America."

"You mean to fetch his ward across with him, Jack?"

"Yes, just to use Bessie as a lever to compel her mother to give up those valuable papers. I always said, you remember, Tom, that man was hugging some secret to his heart. And so he was."

"He's been treating Bessie badly then, half starving her, I think you said?" continued Tom.

"Just what he has, poor girl," growled his chum, savagely. "It's an awful thing to be hungry! I don't see how any one can stand it. But he hasn't broken the spirit of either of them yet, though Bessie's getting so weak she finds herself crying every now and then, just as we heard her. And it was that which brought us over to find out what it meant. But Tom, tell her we mean to stand by, and see that both her mother and herself are taken to a place of safety."

This Tom readily did, though as yet he could hardly understand just how their promise could be fulfilled. One they might manage to take aloft with them, by crowding, but the Caudron was not capable of seating four; nor would it be safe to carry a couple of inexperienced passengers along with themselves.

"But we're losing valuable time," he observed. "The sooner we get in touch with Mrs. Gleason the better. There's a whole lot to be done before we can say we're on the safe side of the fence."

"Then first of all we'd better climb inside the room, hadn't we?" suggested Jack.

In answer Tom proceeded to get one leg over the sill, and then pass his entire body across. Jack quickly followed. In the semi-darkness, for the moon gave a dim light, they clustered there, and continued to map out their immediate plans in whispers that could not have been heard a dozen feet distant.

It appeared that Bessie knew where her mother was confined, though both doors were fastened on the outside to prevent their having communication. But the girl had found a way. Night after night she was accustomed to slipping from her window, when everything was quiet below and the lights all out, making her way along that narrow coping, or ledge, and tapping softly at the window of her mother's room.

They would remain together until toward morning, when the girl made it a practice to return by the same perilous route.

On this particular night it had seemed as though the lights below would never go out. Carl Potzfeldt, the master spy, expecting important news and a messenger from the headquarters of the Crown Prince, had been waiting up until long after midnight in order to fullfil the important duties entrusted to him.

Jack suggested that he creep along that coping and inform the lady of the golden chance for escape that had arrived. But as she would hardly be able to return by the same way, it seemed as though some other scheme must be considered.

Bessie herself had a brilliant thought bordering on an inspiration.

"Listen, and I will tell you," she said at this juncture. "All the time I have been here my one thought has been of escape. I dreamed nothing else save getting my poor mother away from the clutches of that coward who had hypnotized her in the past, and made her believe he was a good man as well as her cousin from Alsace-Lorraine. And I know of a way it can be done."

"Tell us your plan, please," begged Jack; though he would be sorry to learn that the honor of releasing Bessie's imprisoned mother was not to fall to his share in the undertaking.

"There is another window. It opens upon a hallway; and I can get through it, because I've tried it more than once. But the proper time hadn't come, for how were we to flee from this awful country? Wait for me here, both of you. I shall be able to open her barred door, and then my own. And it is better that I carry her the good news than some one who would be a stranger to my mother, however much I have told her about you."

Tom saw that her plan was the best, after all. He himself had been a little afraid that if Jack came tapping at the window of Mrs. Gleason's room she might take the alarm, thinking it but another twist to the odious schemes of Potzfeldt, and perhaps shrieking out in terror, which would cause an alarm, and ruin everything.

Bessie climbed nimbly out of the window,

showing how accustomed she was to such athletic exercises. Jack held on to her to the last, and his whispers were all of an entreating character, as he begged her to be very careful, and not slip in her excitement.

Now she was gone, and the two air service boys, left by themselves in that room of the old Lorraine château, counted the seconds and the minutes until they should hear a gentle signal at the door, to signify that Bessie and her mother were there, about to enter.

Jack walked softly up and down, like a velvet-footed tiger in its cage. He was so worked up by the excitement of the occasion that Tom did not have the heart to ask him to stop his movements, though he certainly would have done so had not the other been keeping on his tiptoes all the while.

What a remarkable turn their venture into the country back of the enemy's lines had taken! And what astounding discoveries they had made in the bargain!

Jack was getting more and more impatient. Several times did he pause at the door, to lay his ear close to the heavy panel, and listen. He wondered what could be keeping Bessie. Surely she had had ample time to open the door of her mother's room and explain everything to the lady. In his excitement he

IN THE OLD LORRAINE CHÂTEAU 179

pictured all sorts of fresh trouble as having befallen the girl. What if by accident she had run across the master German spy in the corridor? But then, in such a case, Bessie surely would have screamed in order to warn her two friends that they were in danger of being discovered, should Potzfeldt and some of his assistants burst into the room.

Of course Jack had magnified things wonderfully. Less than half the time had elapsed than he thought had passed when there came a soft scratching on the door to notify them Bessie was there. They next heard a slight creaking sound, and then the soft closing of the door.

"Bessie, is it you?" asked the eager Jack, softly.

A reply in the affirmative followed.

"And here is mother with me," added the girl, a note of joy in her voice, even though she spoke in a whisper.

So they came together. In the semi-darkness the boys could not see what Bessie's mother looked like. They did note, however, that she was small of stature; and this fact pleased Tom very much indeed. For already he had figured out just how the rescue must be carried out, since there seemed to be no other way.

His plans would entail some sacrifice on Jack's part, and also more or less exposure to peril; but then Tom knew his chum too well to imagine he would hesitate even a moment when called upon to take this additional burden on his shoulders.

Both of them squeezed the trembling hand of the woman, and as best they were able assured her that they meant to carry both Bessie and herself to a place of safety, provided they were courageous enough to trust themselves to the care of two air pilots.

CHAPTER XXII

FACING MORE DIFFICULTIES

"As for me," spoke up Bessie, immediately, just as Jack felt positive she would, "I'd like nothing better. I've been up once in a hydroairplane, and would have gone many times if mother had allowed me."

The lady did not seem to anticipate having a very delightful time of it, for Tom felt her shudder; but she was courageous, and evidently ready to attempt any hazard in order to gain her freedom.

"If only there is some way to fasten me securely," she told them, "I am willing to do anything you say, my brave boys. So make your plans without regard to my feelings in the matter."

Jack about this time evidently began to scent something with regard to Tom's intuitions; at least his word implied a growing skepticism concerning their ability to find room for two passengers aboard a plane intended only for a pilot and an observer, or a gunner.

"Of course one could squeeze in alongside me, Tom," he mentioned hesitatingly; "but do you think it's wise to have anybody with you?

Mightn't it interfere with the working of the controls, and add to the danger?"

"It certainly would, Jack; and that's why I'm forced to call on you to make a sacrifice."

"Go on and say what's on your mind, then," demanded Jack. "No matter what it's going to be, you'll find me ready and willing for anything."

"You'll have to wait for the second trip," Tom announced.

"All right, just as you say, Tom. When will that be, later on to-night?"

"If it's possible to get back, yes," said the other.

"But if you can't make it, then to-morrow night, Tom?"

Jack was not overcome with fear, even though the prospect did appear anything but cheerful. Bessie listened to this low talk, and gave evidence of growing anxiety.

"But why should this be necessary?" she put in at that juncture. "I can stay behind just as well as not. Then perhaps another night later on you could come again, and take me with you to the French lines, and safety."

Jack sniffed in disdain.

"Well, I guess not, Bessie!" he told her, almost sternly. "I'd just like to see myself sailing away, and leaving you here to stand the racket. No, both of you are going to accompany Tom. I can find a hiding place somewhere around; and besides, no one will suspect that an American flier is hanging out here. There's only one thing I hate like everything to think of."

"And I can guess what that is," Tom said, quickly. "You dread to contemplate a long eatless day before you. That's the worst punishment anyone could hand out to you, Jack."

"As far as that goes," interrupted Bessie; "I can tell Jack where the pantry window lies. As the catch is broken you can easily climb in through it later on to-night, and lay in a supply of food. There is always something there. Before that bad man shut me up he tried to starve me, and I stole food myself. Then he guessed what was happening, for he fastened my door, and only allowed me to walk in the grounds in company with a woman he has for a housekeeper."

Thereupon Bessie gave Jack minute directions how to find the window leading into the storeroom. Thus armed the young aviator felt that he ought to be able to stand it, in case his comrade found it impracticable to return on the same night.

"Since all that is fixed," remarked Tom, "it

strikes me we had better get out of this place quickly. Can you lead us down by way of the stairs, Bessie?"

"Oh, yes; for I know every foot of the way," she told him without hesitation. "You see, I expected that some time we would have to slip away by stealth; and so I made myself familiar with everything, even to the fastenings of the great front door, with its chain and catch."

"Then we're in great luck," Jack observed, while Tom on his part went on to ask further.

"All seems dark outside now, Bessie; would that indicate your jailer has gone to his bed? And do you happen to know where his apartment is? That might mean a whole lot to us, you understand."

"I don't believe he ever does really go to bed," she replied. "Once I heard him complain that there were so many times during the night that messengers came from headquarters with demands, or after information expected from over the lines, that he had to secure his sleep while fully dressed, and by throwing himself down on a Turkish lounge he has in his room."

"Well, so long as his sleep is sound it's little we care how or when he gets it," announced Jack, flippantly. "And when you give the word, Tom, we'll all be ready to follow Bessie down the stairs."

FACING MORE DIFFICULTIES 185

Tom was even opening his mouth to say there was really nothing to detain them, if Bessie and her mother had secured what trifles they wished to take away, but after all he did not speak the words that were on his lips.

Through the open window they suddenly heard the sound of heavy, guttural voices. They seemed to come from the road near the entrance gates.

Tom stepped over to the window and looked out. What he saw gave him an unpleasant feeling. There were lights already on the crooked driveway, and a number of men seemed to be advancing in a group.

Jack at his elbow was also staring, and grinding his teeth with anger.

"Hang the luck, I say!" he gritted. "That fresh bunch of Boche officers is bound to knock our plans silly. They'll stir things up again, and we can't get away. Then perhaps some one will discover the doors of the two rooms are unfastened, and that'll start a hornet's nest about our ears."

"Get down, and keep hidden, Jack," urged his companion. "They have lights with them, and might see us as they come along. There's a general, at least, in the lot, that big stout man in the center, and I imagine those other officers belong to his staff."

"But what are they walking for?" whispered Jack, incredulously. "German officers in the High Command don't often tramp along the roads like that, do they?"

"They may have broken down in their car; and learning they were close to this house have come on here to wait till repairs are made. Lots of them know Potzfeldt, I suppose, and one of these men may have been here before on business. The worst of it all is we'll have to give up our scheme of going down by way of the stairs."

They crouched down and watched as best they could, while the half-dozen men in the gray-green uniforms of German officers, and with many decorations on the breast of the martial-looking commander, approached the château's front door.

Already lights had sprung up on the lower floor. Undoubtedly Potzfeldt had heard his unexpected guests coming, and was bestirring himself to welcome them, though inwardly raving over having his rest so frequently disturbed.

He met them at the door, and there ensued more or less talking, all of it in the choicest of German. Again Jack felt sorry that his education was so incomplete that he could only guess at what most of it meant.

FACING MORE DIFFICULTIES 187

Still, Tom could pick up a little of what was said. There was certainly mention made of an unfortunate accident to a car, that would necessitate a delay of some hours for repairs, possibly until morning. The general did not altogether fancy sitting in the car for hours in the cool night air. Especially was this the case after he had learned that there was a house half a mile or so further on where food and drink could be obtained in plenty, if only they chose to walk that far.

All of the newcomers had by now stalked inside the house, and the coast seemed to be clear, so far as those above could see. But down below there was much hurrying to and fro, which would indicate that Potzfeldt must have aroused his retainers, and they were running up and down from wine-cellar to dining-room, bearing acceptable refreshments for the unbidden guests.

"Say, I wonder if that old stout chap could be Hindenburg himself?" Jack whispered in his chum's ear. "I noticed that Mr. Potzfeldt seemed mighty obsequious, as if he felt highly honored at having such a noble visitor, and nothing could be too good to set before him."

"Well, I wouldn't be surprised if you'd hit the nail on the head when you said that, Jack," the other told him. "He was a big, burly man, with a mighty important air about him; and he wore a mustache such as we've always seen in pictures of Hindenburg. But no matter, it doesn't concern us at all, if we can find a way to get down from here."

"Only," said Jack, whimsically, "I do hope if they've got their German appetites along, they don't clean out that pantry before I get my look-in, that's all. Twenty-four hours without a single bite would be the limit for me. I don't think I'd survive the ordeal. Now what, Tom?"

Tom was looking out again.

"That's lucky," Jack heard him mutter.

"Of course it is. But tell me what you're referring to, Tom."

"Some clouds have come along. One is right now covering the face of the moon, you notice. Well, if we are forced to lower Bessie and her mother from the window by means of a rope made from knotted bed-sheets, we stand a chance to avoid being discovered at work by any one who might happen to be abroad just then."

Jack chuckled as though pleased.

"Sure, that's the game, Tom! I knew you'd be equal to getting up some sort of clever scheme. And I'll start in right away making that rope. We want to be certain it's strong enough to bear their weight, that's all."

"I'll help you at the job," Tom told him, for he too wished to be positive about the twisted parts of the sheets, before trusting the girl and her mother to their care.

Fortunately they found that Carl Potzfeldt had some of the airs of a millionaire about him. The sheets were of stout linen, instead of the customary cotton to which the American boys were accustomed. When these were cut first with a sharp pocket-knife, and then torn into long strips about a foot or so in width, they could be twisted and knotted until the result was a novel rope of at least twenty feet in length.

Neither Bessie nor her mother said a single word. They seemed more than willing to be thus lowered to the ground. Such a novel experience might not be delightful, but it amounted to very little when compared with what they had suffered at the hands of their rude and cruel captor.

Soon the odd rope was ready for use.

"Let me be the first to go down," Bessie then said to Tom, in an authoritative voice.

As he had been about to propose the same thing he made not the least objection, but proceeded to secure one end of the strange rope around her body just below the arms, Bessie herself assisting in the operation.

Before attempting the task, Tom stood at the window listening for some little time. He wished to make sure that none of the German officers had remained outside. Tom also meant to satisfy himself that there was no lurking form among the bushes on that side of the château, since the light streaming from the lower windows dissipated some of the advantages gained by the temporary clouding of the moon.

CHAPTER XXIII

LEFT BEHIND IN THE ENEMY COUNTRY

Tom appeared finally to be satisfied, for he turned around to Bessie.

"Now if you're ready we'll lower you safely," he told her.

The girl showed considerable nimbleness in climbing over the window-sill. Jack insisted in having a hand in dropping her slowly down. It was not far, and in a few breaths the girl had reached the solid ground. She understood what was expected of her, and immediately cast off the rude rope, so it might be drawn up and made to serve once more.

Mrs. Gleason showed just as much bravery as her daughter, and was also lowered without trouble.

"You go down next, Tom," whispered Jack. "Then I'll draw it up, and can join you easily enough without the help of the rope. A white thing like this dangling here would be sure to attract attention, if any one came around the corner of the house, and might cost us dearly in the end."

Tom understood. He preferred being the last to stay, but since Jack had taken that upon himself, and was moreover adept at scaling walls, it was folly to dispute his right.

So down Tom went. He had hardly landed when the sheet-rope was swiftly drawn up, and vanished within the room. After that Jack was seen making his way down over the same route he had taken while ascending.

Soon they were all together again, and their queer exit from the room seemed not to have been discovered, for which they felt very thankful indeed.

Tom led the way into the friendly bushes close by. It was his intention to skirt the carriage-drive, as it might contain elements of danger for them. Once they had passed out on the main road to Metz, it would not take them long to reach the field where the big Caudron airplane lay like an exhausted and enormous bat, awaiting their coming to spring into activity.

In passing along they were enabled to catch a glimpse of the interior of the dining-room where Carl Potzfeldt was entertaining his distinguished visitor to the best of his ability in those times when scarcity ruled.

Tom managed to get a better look at the general. He was more than ever convinced that the big man with the strong features and all these decorations on his uniform, was in fact Hindenburg, the head of the whole German army, whose opinion carried even more weight with the people just then than that of Kaiser Wilhelm.

It would be something worth while to be able to say they had been within a dozen feet of the famous commander, the Iron Man of Germany. Tom vaguely wished he had some means of capturing the general then and there, and carrying him over the lines to the French headquarters. That would indeed be a feat well worth praise from General Petain; but of course it was utterly impossible.

They gained the gate, and there Tom insisted on looking carefully around so as to make doubly certain that no sentinel had been left on duty while General Hindenburg remained within the house.

When this fact was made clear he led the way forth. The little party of four almost ran along the road, so eager were they to place as much ground as possible between themselves and the seat of danger.

There was always a chance that the flight of Bessie and her mother might be discovered by some one connected with the household, and communicated to Potzfeldt. He, of course, would exhaust every means in trying to overtake the fugitives.

But Tom chuckled while telling himself that they must needs have extraordinary and fleet steeds who could successfully pursue those who had trusted their safety to his care and that of the big Caudron airplane.

Jack hardly knew where the field lay, having become "rattled," as he called it, from the adventures at the château. So after all it was fortunate that Tom had taken his bearings as well as he had. He knew just when to leave the road, and start across the open space. Then the lone tree began to loom up, for the moon had once more thrust her face from behind the enveloping cloud.

"It's all right, Bessie," said Jack reassuringly. "Our plane lies close to the foot of that tree ahead there. If all goes well you'll be on your way before many minutes have passed."

"Thanks to you, Jack," murmured the girl admiringly.

"Shucks! that isn't a circumstance to what I'd be willing to do for you and your mother!" Jack boldly told her.

"But all the same it is very brave of you, Jack, and I can never forget your kindness to us," she insisted. "I hope and pray that nothing terrible will happen to you while we're gone, and that I'll soon see you again."

"I hope so too, Bessie," he chuckled, as if

amused. "As to anything happening to me, I guess I know how to hide all right. The worst that can knock me is getting a little mite hungry, you know. If that big German general and his staff leave a bite in the pantry I'm going after it, believe me! Then I'll find a hole, and crawl in, somewhere close by here, so I can watch for Tom's return."

Apparently Jack had mapped his whole programme out; and it seemed that an adequate supply of provisions occupied the most prominent place in them.

They were now at the spot where the Caudron had been left. Tom's mind was eased of the secret fears he had entertained when he saw the machine was still where they had left it. So far as he could tell no one had been near to meddle with it.

First of all Bessie and her mother must be fastened securely to the seat where Jack had sat on the trip to Metz. Tom, like a wise general, had provided himself with plenty of the strips of linen from the torn sheets. This he utilized in tying the passengers, so that there would not be the slightest chance of their falling out.

Even if Mrs. Gleason should faint through terror on finding herself a mile up in the air, she could not fall out of the machine. But

Tom entertained high hopes that both of his passengers were going to display extraordinary courage, and give him no cause at all for anxiety.

Jack tried to assist in the operation, but his hands were trembling so with the excitement that Tom pushed him away.

"Leave the job to me, Jack," he told the other. "Too many cooks spoil the broth, you know. I'll make everything secure, depend on it."

"Of course I know you will, Tom," the other hastened to assure him. "Perhaps it is better only one handled the business. And Bessie—"

"Yes, Jack," said the girl, slipping a hand out toward him, which Jack took in his, and pressed reassuringly.

"Don't bother your head for a single minute about me, mind. I'll be all right, and perhaps able to join you again this very night. It's a great lark for me, and I wouldn't miss it for a heap. But oh, if only we could kidnap that big commander, and carry him over to have an interview with General Petain, how proud I'd be!"

Tom smiled on realizing that the same idea had occurred to Jack that had flashed through his own mind.

"Here, take my automatic, Jack," Tom said.

"You may find occasion to use it before I come back."

The other complied, and apparently he felt more confidence, once he knew he had in his possession the means for defending himself should any ordinary danger threaten. Tom was loath to depart, once he had everything arranged. The truth of the matter was he hated to leave his chum in the enemy country; it seemed as though he were deserting him.

So he "fiddled" around, testing this wire guy, and using his electric hand torch to give him light, so he could once more run his eye over the motor on which he had been working.

"Come, Tom, it's no use hanging around here a minute longer," Jack had finally to tell him. "Get aboard and I'll spin your wheel for you and give you a boost for a start. Then I'll drop out of sight, because some of them may run this way when they hear the clatter and guess the cause."

Tom climbed to his seat and settled himself according to his customary thorough manner. He tried the controls, and was not satisfied until he had tested everything within reach.

"Say when, Tom!" Jack remarked, having finally left Bessie's side and gone to the propellers of the big plane.

Tom drew in a long breath. He knew he

had a risky venture ahead, taking those two inexperienced passengers over the hostile lines, possibly amidst showers of exploding shrapnel shells. But it was not this that weighed so heavily on his spirits. He felt almost like a criminal at leaving Jack behind.

"All right; let her go!" he announced grimly.

There came a sudden whirring sound. Then the loud hum of the motors chimed in, and the big Caudron machine started off.

"Good-bye, Tom! Good-bye, Bessie!" Jack was heard saying, although the noise of the plane almost drowned his voice.

Faster they went now, as the machine gained momentum. Tom paid strict attention to his business of pilot. At just the proper time he must elevate the forward rudder, which would cause the plane to leave the ground and start upward at a sharp angle.

Jack stood gazing after the object that was quickly growing more and more indistinct in the dim moonlight, gazing with a strange heaviness in the region of his heart. He had to shut his teeth firmly together to conquer the momentary weakness that threatened to overpower him. But his resolution remained master of the field.

"If only he gets them safely across," Jack muttered to himself, when he could no longer see the airplane, though its noisy working came plainly to his ears, "it'll be all right. But they've heard the racket over at the house, too, I guess, because men are shouting, and I can see lights flashing this way and that."

When he discovered that men with lanterns were actually looking around as if to learn where the departing airplane could have been resting, and what it all meant, Jack concluded it was time to conceal himself.

CHAPTER XXIV

TROUBLOUS TIMES FOR JACK

THE men bearing the lanterns came closer, Jack saw, as he himself scurried amidst the bushes seeking a hiding-place.

"Guess that Potzfeldt must know that planes can drop down on his big open field," the youth muttered to himself. Then as a new idea flashed through his brain he continued: "Whee! I warrant you now that ours wasn't the first airplane to land there. Sometimes maybe the spy he wants to send back of the French lines gets aboard right here, with his little cage of homers."

Presently loud exclamations told that the men had discovered the marks of the arriving and departing Caudron machine. Jack could hear them exchanging remarks about it, in German of course. Then he saw one of the trio start back toward the house. He was half running, as though much excited. Jack jumped to a conclusion.

"Say," he said to himself, in a whisper, as though even the sound of his own voice might be company for him, "now that must have been Carl Potzfeldt himself. What's he making for the house with a hop, skip and jump for? Perhaps one of his sharp-eyed men has told him there are marks of small shoes around; and old Carl got a sudden suspicion something tremendous has happened."

The master-spy came back again. He was now accompanied by two others, and Jack saw by their uniforms that they were members of the general's staff.

All were talking earnestly, Potzfeldt, Jack imagined, telling them some story concerning Bessie and her mother, in which he figured as a noble man, trying to save Mrs. Gleason from the wiles of some American fortune hunter, into whose hands he now feared she and her daughter had fallen.

"My! but he's wild!" chuckled the hidden observer. "He realizes that the two American boys have been too much for his scheming after all. Guess he must have had a suspicion all along we'd break up his game. That'd account for his plotting with the other spy to have our planes meddled with, so we'd meet with some terrible accident that would remove us from his path."

Jack was really enjoying himself. It did him good to hear Potzfeldt raging around, and spluttering as though his rage half choked him.

What Bessie had said concerning the cruel

treatment she had received at the hands of her mother's relative had fired Jack's blood. He detested a man who in order to accumulate money could treat a helpless woman and girl as Potzfeldt had those who were in his power.

"I'd just like," he was telling himself as he listened, "to be one of three fellows who had that villain in their power, with a nice big kettle of hot tar handy, ditto three feather pillows. Oh, wouldn't we make him a queer bird, though! The extinct dodo'd have nothing on him, believe me! But it's fine to hear him raging around like that. I only wish Bessie could listen."

After a time Potzfeldt and his men went away. They knew they could do nothing, as the big enemy plane had long since departed, and must by then be many miles on the return journey to the French lines.

An hour went by and all seemed quiet in the region of the big house by the side of the road. Jack had not forgotten the promise made to himself. It might mean additional danger, to be sure; but when he thought of a long day ahead, in all probability, with an empty stomach constantly reproaching him, he felt equal to the task.

He had no trouble in finding the entrance to the grounds. Everything seemed quiet, as though the general and his staff were endeavoring to get a little sleep before resuming their journey to the fighting front.

Jack was soon under the window that had been described to him by Bessie. It gave light to the pantry during the daytime. Also he had been assured, the catch that secured it was broken, so that if he were bold enough he could easily gain entrance and take his pick of what the housekeeper had stored there.

Such a nimble chap as Jack had no difficulty whatever in making an entrance. Finding himself within the big closet, he listened, and, hearing no sound, struck a match.

By the light thus afforded he could see what lay within his reach. Trust one with an empty stomach for knowing what he wants under such conditions. Jack immediately commenced to gather together a supply of food of various kinds, such as could be eaten without need for a fire.

Quantity rather than quality seemed to rule his actions. At any rate, when he gathered his spoils together he had quite enough to last an ordinary man several days.

"Well," he told himself, when lifting the bundle he had made. "I may be marooned around here a long time, and never get another chance at this supply station. I believe in striking while the iron's hot. Now to get it outside without raising a crowd."

It was indeed a lucky thing that there was no watch-dog at the Potzfeldt place. Undoubtedly this was because of the many visitors coming and going at all times, who might be bothered by a savage beast.

Jack managed to get back safely to the nest where he had hidden at the time of the excitement, when Potzfeldt and his men were in the field. He gave a sigh of relief after it was all over.

Soon the young aviator settled down to try to get some sleep, as some time still remained before dawn would break. He meant to be early astir. There was danger in the air, as he might be discovered unless he arranged for a better hiding place than the covert of bushes where he now lay.

Whether his sleep was worth while, or rendered uneasy by dreams, Jack never told. He was awake though, when the sun peeped above the horizon, and began to bestir himself. Presently people would be moving about. Some of the men might even come out to the open field again, to look at the telltale marks. And if they chanced to suspect that one of the crew of the Caudron had been left behind, a hasty search was apt to reveal his presence.

Accordingly Jack commenced to retire deeper into the wood, and managed by great care to cover his tracks fairly well in so doing. Finally he found a place that seemed to him about as good as anything he might expect to run across; and so he crawled into the bushes again.

Then he had a most pleasing task to start upon, which was nothing more nor less than that of appeasing his appetite, never more voracious, he fancied, than just then. Without a twinge of conscience regarding the fact that it was stolen food he disposed of, Jack commenced his morning meal.

"I'm only enjoying some of the good stuff that scoundrel deprived Bessie of," he told himself, with a grin of contentment, after he had eaten until he could not take another bite. "Besides, everything is fair in war-times. When you're raiding through the enemy's country it's supposed you'll live on the spoils around you. Well, I'm going to live, and Carl Potzfeldt is my enemy, all right. He's proved that in a dozen different ways."

That idea set him to thinking about Bessie again, how she had taken such a queer way to try to warn him, after overhearing her guardian plotting with one of his men the injury to one or both of the young Americans.

"Now I wonder," Jack mused, as he lay in

perfect peace with the world, for he had eaten his fill, "how he knew we had joined the Lafayette Escadrille. But then those German spies learn a lot of things, and he may have been keeping tabs on Tom and me right along. Deep down in his heart he suspected we'd bother him, and so he wanted to get us before we had a chance to strike. Well, the shoe is on the other foot, it seems."

The morning advanced. Fortunately it proved to be a fair day for so early in April. Had a storm arisen Jack might have found it hard to find shelter. As it was, all he had to do was to lie under the bushes and doze from time to time.

Whenever he got to thinking of Tom a queer feeling came over him. It made him uneasy, though he could not explain why that should be so; and from time to time he took himself to task for being worried.

"Of course Tom got back safe and sound," he would muse. "He's too clever a pilot to make a bad job of such a business. And yet, if he doesn't come to-night I'll be terribly anxious. Oh, forget all that! will you, Jack Parmly? Think of something pleasant now. For instance, that it's nearly high noon, and most folks lunch then."

He had just calmed down again, when he

had a sudden chill. Men were working in a field about three hundred yards away, for he could hear them calling to one another in German.

Suddenly there came a series of snappy barks. Jack looking around was horrified to discover a small dog. It was a dachschund, long of body, and with crooked, bandy legs. It was standing before the hidden boy and evidently bent on telling everybody by his barks that some suspicious person was hiding in the bushes.

It was a crisis that made Jack's blood run cold!

CHAPTER XXV
BACK TO SAFETY — CONCLUSION

JACK hardly knew what to do. He made threatening gestures at the dog, but they, of course, only added to the trouble, for the animal renewed his barking more briskly than ever.

Then Jack had an inspiration, such as sometimes comes when all seems lost. If the dog continued his barking, sooner or later one of the men working in the field not far off would have his curiosity aroused, and come to ascertain what sort of wild animal the dog had treed.

Jack unfastened his package of food. Since stern tactics had no effect he meant to try to make friends with the dachschund. Dogs are always more or less hungry, he argued; and this must be especially true at that time in every part of Germany, Alsace-Lorraine not excepted, since the pinch of two-and-a-half years of war had made terrible inroads on all kinds of food.

Jack commenced to eat. The dog kept on barking, though not quite so savagely now. The smell of the food had reached him, and he would occasionally give a little imploring whine between his barks.

So Jack spoke to him in a soft, wheedling tone. Then he held up a scrap of meat, and caught the eager attention of the little beast; after which he tossed it to him. It vanished like a flash. The dog even wagged his tail, as if to let the man know his animosity was quickly giving way to interest. Surely any one who had all that food along with him could not be a suspicious personage.

The next scrap fell a little short, and the dog advanced to get it. So by degrees Jack tempted him, until in the end he was patting the squatty animal on the back, and still feeding him. They were now the best of friends. Kindness had accomplished what all the threatening gestures, supplemented with many sticks hurled at the beast, could never have brought about.

Jack believed he had saved himself from discovery. He could easily understand what hardships must have awaited him had he ever fallen into the hands of Carl Potzfeldt.

The afternoon went by very tediously. The dog came and went, staying for short periods with Jack. The vast store of food was a magnet that held the little beast fast. It had doubtless been a long time since he had had his full.

By degrees the day waned, and evening came along.

Jack never saw the sun set with less regret

than he did on that occasion. Still he knew that long hours must pass before the moon would peep in view above the eastern horizon.

As he sat, he allowed his thoughts to roam backward. Once more in imagination he could see his friends who were on the other side of the ocean. Then for a change he would take another "snack," as he called it, for lack of anything else to occupy his attention.

Several times also he dozed, but always arousing with a start at some sound, under the impression that it might be Tom who had come, and, not finding him, gone away again.

Finally he began to believe it must surely be past midnight; and the late moon would presently be making an appearance. On looking closely toward the east he became aware that the heavens were betraying such a fact, for a distinct silvery glow was beginning to appear, low down.

Then came a streak of light. It was the moon. Slowly she mounted higher, as if more or less ashamed of the dilapidated appearance of her usually smiling face.

Jack had earlier in the night changed his place of lodging. He again occupied his former quarters close to the spot where he and Tom had landed when they wished to overhaul the motor that was acting so badly.

BACK TO SAFETY—CONCLUSION

The minutes dragged.

Then once more Jack bent his head, and put a hand up to his ear to listen. He laughed to himself with glee.

"That's Tom coming!" he muttered joyously. "I knew Tom wouldn't fail me. All the same I'll be mighty glad when I'm aboard the plane and on the air route to Bar-le-Duc and my own cot."

Louder grew the sounds. There could not be the slightest doubt about it now, Jack decided. A plane was coming at top speed, and keeping not a great distance above the treetops of the little valley in which the house of Carl Potzfeldt and the road to Metz lay.

Louder grew the insistent drumming. Jack wondered whether some of those at the château might not also hear the racket, and, guessing what it would mean, hasten out to the field in time to give Tom and himself a volley of shots.

Now the plane was coming, like a great condor of the Andes about to alight on a mountain peak. Jack gauged full well where it would land. He ran with all his might to be close to the spot. The less time wasted in getting him aboard the better for their safety, he believed, remembering what cause Carl Potzfeldt now had for being suspicious when a plane visited his meadow.

BACK TO SAFETY—CONCLUSION

Then the big Caudron ran along the ground and came to a full stop.

"Jack!"

"Yes, Tom, I'm here, and mighty glad to see you!" cried the lad who had counted the minutes until his brain seemed to reel with the strain.

"Get aboard in a hurry, Jack. We've no time to waste here."

"I know that even better than you do," returned the other.

There was indeed need of haste. The air service boys could hear voices from where the château was located. Someone had heard the humming of the oncoming airplane. It was Potzfeldt himself, and now he and two of his men came hurrying out on the field, all armed with pistols.

Jack only waited to give the propellers a whirl, and then, as the motor took up its work, he made a leap for his seat. Oh, how good it seemed to be once more in that airplane!

"Stop! Stop!" roared a guttural voice in German. "Stop, or we fire!"

Now the airplane was moving along the ground, bumping and rocking considerably. But Tom knew how to manage, and presently the plane commenced to soar slowly upward.

Loud and angry voices announced the fact that Carl Potzfeldt had arrived close enough to get a view of the rising plane in the misty light of the moon.

"Stop! I command you! Stop!" roared the German. And then came the crack! crack! crack! of firearms.

The air service boys, because of the noise of the motor, did not hear the discharge of the pistols, but suddenly Jack heard the spatter of a bullet as it struck the machine close beside him. Then he ducked and made a motion to Tom to let his chum know that they were under fire.

But the machine was gaining headway rapidly, and presently they were so high that those below could no longer reach them. Up and up they went until they were thousands of feet above the valley that had been the scene of this remarkable adventure.

Tom headed back along the course he had just come. It was now easy to pick up one landmark after another, and in due course of time they passed over the lines once more. Of course, the sound of the plane's propellers was heard by the Germans, and some shrapnel was sent after them; but as Tom was careful to keep high in the air, this did not reach them, and soon they were out of the danger belt.

Fifteen minutes later they made a landing, this time on the well remembered aviation field of Bar-le-Duc. Here there were attendants on hand ready to care for the machines.

"Glad to see you got back," said one of the attendants, grinning. He knew that Tom had gone off on the second trip to bring Jack.

The two air service boys found a car to take them to the villa. The long ride through the night air had made both of them very sleepy, and yet neither felt just then like retiring.

"It's a lucky thing, Tom," said Jack, between yawns, "that I had this fur-lined pilot's coat along with me. Only for that I'd have been mighty cold out there in the open last night, with no chance for a fire."

"Well, it's all past now, Jack. Tell me what happened to you during my absence."

Jack, was nothing loath, and as quickly as possible gave his chum the particulars of how he had gone into hiding and almost been betrayed by the dog.

Tom had already told Jack about what had become of Mrs. Gleason and Bessie. They had been taken to a house some miles back of the lines, and were to be made comfortable there for the night.

"And early in the morning they are to start for Paris," Tom said with satisfaction. "I

BACK TO SAFETY—CONCLUSION 215

managed through our captain to get them passage aboard a train that is to take some wounded back to the base hospitals. Mrs. Gleason says she means to stay in Paris and help all she can as a Red Cross nurse, for she has had some experience in nursing."

"That's fine!" was Jack's comment. And then for the time being he became somewhat silent.

Tom could easily understand that his chum was cherishing a hope that some time or other when they were taking a vacation from their arduous duties while flying for France, the pair of them might visit the French metropolis, and if so they would certainly try to see Bessie and her mother again.

"And I've got more news to tell," remarked Tom, when the pair were about to turn in for their much-needed sleep. "You'll remember about that message we found in the capsule on the leg of the homing pigeon. Well, one of the other pigeons we found was used to send a false message to the Germans, telling them that a certain part of the French line was very weak. A short while later the Germans made a furious attack on that part of the line, and, believe me, they caught it for fair — the plucky French soldiers, aided by the artillery, literally wiped up the ground with them."

"That's great news!" cried Jack. "Then it paid to bring down that pigeon, didn't it?"

"It sure did, Jack!"

Two days later came a most important announcement, especially to the American airmen.

"Things are coming our way at last," the valiant commander announced, as they crowded about him. "The papers this morning say that Uncle Sam has at last got his back up. Any day may now bring the glorious news from across the Atlantic, telling that the United States has taken the steps that will put her in this World War against the Central Powers. Then it will be all over but the shouting."

"That's right!" cried Jack.

"You just leave it to Uncle Sam to do it!" added Tom.

Many more adventures were in store for the young aviators, and what some of them were will be related in the next volume of this series, to be entitled "Air Service Boys Over the Rhine; Or, Fighting Above the Clouds."

And here for the present let us leave the air service boys and say good-bye.

THE END

HERE'S WHAT PEOPLE ARE SAYING ABOUT LAURA PETHERBRIDGE AND STEPFAMILIES OF THE BIBLE

"Laura Petherbridge has created yet another work that offers practical insights for building a loving and safe stepfamily. *Stepfamilies of the Bible: Timeless Wisdom for Blended Families* allows us to jump inside the complex world of these biblical families, and their feelings and fears seem strangely familiar. The journey they walk with God is much the same as ours. Discover anew the families we know so well. Or, *thought* we knew so well."

~ **Ron Deal**
Blended family author, speaker, and therapist. President of Smart Stepfamilies™
SmartStepfamilies.com

Laura Petherbridge sheds light on the multi-faceted realities involved in stepfamilies. She offers a pathway to restoration by showing how God reveals Himself in our lives. *Stepfamilies of the Bible* is a unique and much-needed book for blended families who are open to learning lessons from God's Word.

~ **Ken Canfield**, PhD, LPC
Founder of National Center for Fathering and National Association for Grandparenting

"Laura Petherbridge has a heart for those in blended families. *Stepfamilies of the Bible: Timeless Wisdom for Blended Families* is a great, biblical resource to encourage and help you overcome common obstacles you may be facing."

~ **Chris Fabry**
Award-winning author and host of the daily program *Christ Fabry Live* on Moody Radio.

"When we're coaching a blended family, we always utilize Laura Petherbridge's resources. *Stepfamilies of the Bible* is now added to our recommendations! This book is a treasure as it provides biblical examples of how to navigate the good, and the hard, of blending two families into one."

~ **Mark and Jill Savage**
Marriage coaches and authors of *No More Perfect Marriages*

In *Stepfamilies of the Bible*, Laura Petherbridge validates the complex nuances of blended families while pointing to relevant truths that provide a template for healing relationships. She vulnerably shares her own story and masterfully presents insights gleaned from biblical characters who walked through similar challenging blended family dynamics. I highly recommend this book to anyone who needs redemptive hope and a reminder that God always redeems, restores, and rewrites our stories.

~ **Michelle Watson Canfield, PhD, LPC**
Author of *Let's Talk: Conversation Starters for Dads and Daughters* and podcast host of The Dad Whisperer

Laura Petherbridge is an expert on blended families. *Stepfamilies of the Bible* gives insight into biblical families that faced the same challenges you, and those you love, experience. This powerful book substantiates the real issues stepfamilies encounter such as, jealousy, anger, insecurity, fear, and disconnection. Using her childhood experience growing up in a stepfamily, plus her journey as a stepmom, Laura dives into practical tips filled with Bible-based wisdom. This resource reveals how healing, assurance, and unity are within the readers' reach.

~ **Carol Kent**
Founder of Speak Up Ministries, speaker, and author of numerous books, including

When I Lay My Isaac Down, He Holds My Hand, Between a Rock and a Grace Place, and *Becoming a Woman of Influence*

Did you know many heroes in the Bible came from blended families? God is at work in blended families, no matter how complicated. With compassion and insight, Laura Petherbridge writes Stepfamilies of the Bible from her own experiences as a stepchild and then a stepmom. She leads you to biblical hope and healing in every chapter.

~ Arlene Pellicane
Author of *Making Marriage Easier,* host of the Happy Home podcast

StepFamilies of the Bible contains wisdom for all families because it lays a healthy foundation for marriage, family, and the future. God sees you, knows you, knows your life—and He cares! Being in a blended marriage can bring a whirlpool of various emotions. But God, our Creator, can create a path forward for each of us! Laura Petherbridge has gathered timeless truths from the Bible and Biblical characters that will enrich, inspire, and instruct each reader with powerful, practical, productive, positive ideas and illustrations. Laura provides honest and authentic principles and flashing yellow lights that can serve as cautions to avoid. Be a triumphant overcomer, read this book, give this book, and live the principles in this book.

~ Pam and Bill Farrel
Authors of 60 books, including bestselling *Men are Like Waffles, Women are Like Spaghetti.*
Co-Directors of Love-Wise Ministries

Stepfamilies of the Bible is a tender guide, and Laura Petherbridge is an absolute spiritual powerhouse! Anything that flows from her brilliant brain and mighty heart is an indisputable must. Teaching with great humility, wisdom, and compassion, I have witnessed her bring life and healing to families over and over again. Don't miss this!

~ **Allison Allen**
Speaker with Women of Faith, Author of *Thirsty for More, Seen, Secure and Free,* and *Hidden,* Co-Host of Lisa Harper's Back Porch Theology Podcast.

Stepfamilies of the Bible needed to be written, and Laura Petherbridge is the one who needed to write it. Her fresh, bright approach uses blended Bible families to help and guide the modern stepfamily. This resource provides hope and strategies for overcoming relevant and complex stepfamily issues because we no longer need to wonder if God understands the plight of stepfamilies. He does! Matters such as jealousy, bitterness, anger, and favoritism are addressed with honesty and vulnerability. Laura encourages anyone in—or connected to—a blended family. She understands the pain, challenges, and possibilities embedded into each stepfamily and fills the reader with hope of family bonding that is within reach. I've known and worked with her for years. I trust her wisdom.

~ **Dr. Kathy Koch**
Founder of Celebrate Kids, Inc., speaker, author of many parenting books including *Parent Differently* and *8 Great Smarts*

Laura Petherbridge has put in the work to encourage more than 40% of our population with the Truth of God's Word. Does God see me? Does the Bible speak to my current situation of a blended family? We wonder about this more often than we care to admit. Yes, He sees. *Stepfamilies of the Bible* presents this fact beautifully. Sadly, too many pastors ignore blended families because the scenarios are messy, and acknowledging these families is too risky. We are so grateful that Laura Petherbridge addresses these issues and how God sees the pain, hurt, and difficulty of blended families. The trials that blended families face are unique and at times intense—but there is hope. If you're tired of platitudes and disconnected head-nodding when seeking help for your family, read on. We are always amazed at the wisdom and practical insights Laura presents on blended-family dynamics. She is indeed the smart stepmom! *Stepfamilies of the Bible* will equip you to know that the eternal God has spoken about where you are; He sees you.

~ **Will and Meeke Addison**
Authors, speakers, founders of Culture Proof,
Co-hosts of the Culture Proof podcast.

As a Bible lover and teacher, I've feasted on the stories God chose to share in the Bible many times. And yet, I've rarely studied those families through the lens of them being a stepfamily. I'm so grateful that Laura Petherbridge was obedient to God and brought this truth to light. *Stepfamilies of The Bible* unpacks life-transforming lessons through the eyes of familiar Bible families. Laura's hard-earned wisdom is applicable to anyone, not merely stepfamilies. This inspired resource is for anyone who desires healthy relationships, peace in their life, and honor to our God!

~ **Shellie Rushing Tomlinson**
Speaker, author of several books including *Seizing the Good Life*, and Belle of All Things Southern podcast host.
BelleOfAllThingsSouthern.com

I unexpectedly became a stepmother after 50. Laura Petherbridge's insights and resources have been extremely valuable to me. As a relationship and personality expert, I thought life as a stepmother to adult kids would be easy. I was wrong. Her newest book *Stepfamilies of the Bible: Timeless Wisdom for Blended Families* is a fabulous addition to her body of work. It will be a great help to those in a stepfamily, regardless of the age of the stepchildren or stepparents.

~ Marita Littauer
Author of *Wired that Way*; founder
of The Best-Life Project Best-LifeProject.com